A TIMELINE
OF IRISH HISTORY

A TIMELINE
OF IRISH HISTORY

RICHARD KILLEEN

GILL & MACMILLAN

PICTURE CREDITS:

Every effort has been made to contact the copyright holders for images reproduced in this book. The publishers would welcome any errors or omissions being brought to their attention.

Page 6, National Museum of Ireland; 7, National Library of Ireland; 8, Private Collection; 12, Private Collection; 13, Department of the Environment (Northern Ireland); 15, Trinity College, Dublin; 20/21, Gill & Macmillan; 23, Gill & Macmillan; 25, Gill & Macmillan; 26, Gill & Macmillan; 28, Gill & Macmillan; 30, Private Collection; 32, National Library of Ireland; 34, Peter Newark Historical Pictures; 35, Private Collection; 38, Malcolm Porter; 41, Peter Newark Historical Pictures; 42, National Library of Ireland; 43, Peter Newark Historical Pictures; 45, National Portrait Gallery; 46, Department of the Environment (Northern Ireland); 48, Peter Newark Historical Pictures; 50, Peter Newark Historical Pictures; 54, Private Collection; 55, National Library of Ireland; 56, National Museum of Ireland; 57, Private Collection; 58, Irish Image Collection; 59, Gill & Macmillan; 61, Irish Image Collection; 62, Gill & Macmillan; 65, Irish Image Collection; 66, Private Collection; 67, Irish Image Collection; 68, Private Collection; 70, National Library of Ireland; 71, National Gallery of Ireland; 75, Illustrated London News; 78, Irish Image Collection; 79, Hulton Picture Library; 80, Private Collection; 81, National Library of Ireland; 83, National Library of Ireland; 84, Private Collection; 88, Kilmainham Gaol; 91, National Library of Ireland; 93, Hulton Picture Library; 97, Private Collection; 99, Private Collection; 100, Private Collection; 102, Private Collection; 104, Private Collection; 105, National Museum Photo Library.

First published in Ireland, 2003
by Gill & Macmillan Limited, Hume Avenue, Park West, Dublin 12, Ireland
with associated companies throughout the world
www.gillmacmillan.ie

Text copyright © 2003 Richard Killeen

ISBN 978 07171 3484 7

Design, Cartography and Picture Research: Cartographica Limited

Printed in Malaysia

Typeset in Sabon and Trajan

6 5 4 3

INTRODUCTION

There is more to history than dates. Every individual life, let alone the historic lives of the various communities that have inhabited the island of Ireland since antiquity, is more than a catalogue of events. Context is all. And yet without dates, the contexts lack an anchor point.

This book aims to serve a simple purpose: to provide a sequential timeline of the major events of Irish history. It is, therefore, a book of dates. But it also tries to go some way beyond mere dating. I have attempted, where space allows and where the subject warrants it, to give some explanatory context for the course of individual events. In the nature of things, such comments can only be extremely summary but they do make a contribution, however minimal, to the reader's understanding. In addition, the book contains nine short essays which read together provide a condensed narrative of Irish history.

A Timeline of Irish History has no grand theme or interpretation to propose. However, one can only be struck by the effect that events outside Ireland have had on the Irish past. Like all islands, Ireland is engaged in an endless love-hate dialogue with the big neighbours nearby. Since the end of the eighteenth century, that dialogue has taken the form of a desire to shake off the political control exercised by the nearest big neighbour. Well, almost: one corner of the island wanted the nearest big neighbour to stay and so it has. But the political departure of Britain from most of Ireland in 1922 has been paralleled by an ever-increasing influence of British (and Anglo-American) culture. The endless insular dilemma is whether you should concentrate on what sets you apart – roughly what the Republic tried to do in the de Valera years – or whether you should connect with the wider world and borrow from it. In different form, it is the dilemma that Britain itself – another island – faces over its future relations with the European Union. It is a dilemma that has informed much of Irish history. It produces no constant or simple answer.

RK
Dublin
April 2003

Contents

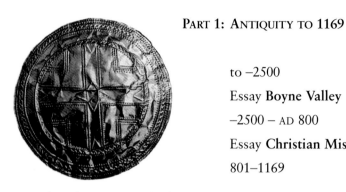

The early Bronze Age also found fine quality examples of gold metal working and ornamentation, such as this gold 'Sun-disc', one of two found at Tedavnet in Co. Monaghan.

Part 1: Antiquity to 1169   **8**

to −2500   8

Essay **Boyne Valley**   9

−2500 − AD 800   12–15

Essay **Christian Missionaries**   16

801–1169   18–21

Part 2: Medieval Ireland   **22**

1170–1250   22–25

Essay **Norman Ireland**   26

1251–1534   28–33

Part 3: Early Modern Ireland   **34**

Essay **Tudor Conquest**   34

1535–1649   36–49

Essay **Cromwell**   50

1650–1740   54–61

Essay **Ascendancy**   62

1741–1775   64–65

PART 4: MODERN IRELAND   66

1778–1829   66–69

Essay **Nationalism**   70

1830–1912   72–83

Essay **Revolution**   84

1913–1969   86–99

Essay **Troubles**   100

1970–2002   104–105

FURTHER READING   106

INDEX   108

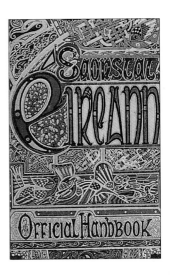

The Official Handbook of the Irish Free State. The cover, by Art O'Murnaghan, is in the traditional style of Celtic manuscript illumination.

ANTIQUITY TO 1169

c. 8000 BC
End of the Ice Age. Beginning of vegetation.

c. 6500 BC
Ireland an island, as rising sea levels divide it from Britain.

5935 BC
Archaeological date of Mesolithic site at Mount Sandel, Co. Derry, earliest evidence of human settlement in Ireland.

c. 4500 BC
Earliest evidence of stone tools, spearheads, axes etc.

c. 4000 BC
Beginnings of agriculture: cultivation of wheat and barley.

c. 3500 BC
Ceide Fields at Belderg, Co. Mayo, the oldest enclosed farmland discovered in Western Europe.

c. 3500 BC
Surviving evidence of Neolitic pottery, basketry and stone and shell ornaments.

c. 3000 BC
Axe factories at Tievebulliagh, Co. Antrim and Brockley on nearby Rathlin Island used porcellanite stone in manufacture of axes that were distributed widely in Britain and Ireland.

c. 3000 BC
First evidence of megalithic tombs, of which the Proleek Dolmen at Ballymascanlon, Co. Louth appears to be one of the oldest.

c. 2500 BC
Newgrange, the most spectacular of the Neolithic Irish passage graves, sited at the bend of the Boyne, Co. Meath, with two other contemporary sites, Knowth and Dowth, nearby.

c. 2500 BC
Approximate date for the Poulnabrone Dolmen, Co. Clare, one of the country's most dramatic Neolithic survivals.

c. 2500 BC
End of Neolithic (New Stone Age) era, as first metals are introduced to Ireland.

Above: The Irish Giant Deer (Megaloceros giganteus) reached its zenith about 12,000 years ago. It stood 2m high at the shoulder or over 3m in the case of males whose antlers spanned around 3m. These were frail and more for show than combat.

Below: At Tievebulliagh, almost a mile up the side of a mountain near Cushendall, Co. Antrim, outcrops of porcellanite were exploited to produce polished axeheads from which a thriving export trade developed. The map shows their distribution as far south as Kent in England.

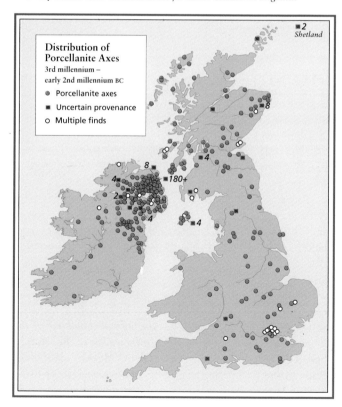

Distribution of Porcellanite Axes
3rd millennium – early 2nd millennium BC
● Porcellanite axes
■ Uncertain provenance
○ Multiple finds

Boyne Valley

THE RIVER BOYNE flows into the Irish Sea about forty kilometres north of Dublin. It rises in the Irish midlands and follows a north-easterly course through the rich limestone pastureland of Co. Meath, picking up the waters of its principal tributary, the Blackwater, at the town of Navan. From there, it gradually turns to the east – wholly so following the small town of Slane. Its port town is Drogheda, at the head of a short estuary.

With the Liffey, the Boyne is the only significant river in the east-central part of Ireland. Neither is as impressive as the four major rivers of the south-eastern corner – the Slaney, Barrow, Nore and Suir. But their historic significance is at least as great. The Liffey flows into Dublin Bay, the most significant safe anchorage on the east coast and the one commanding the quickest crossing to central Britain. The crossing from Wexford, although shorter, delivers one to the wilds of west Wales, whereas the Dublin crossing gave access in Roman times to the town of Chester, in Norman times to the great fortress of Caernarvon and in modern times to Liverpool.

The Boyne, having no anchorage to rival Dublin Bay, did not prosper in the same way. However, its valley has probably seen more continuous civilised settlement than any other identifiable region in Ireland. It has been inhabited from the earliest antiquity and the evidence for the continuity of civilised life along its banks and in its catchment area is abundant.

All civilisation began with settlement: the abandonment of nomadic ways, the domestication of draught animals, the establishment of permanent agricultural settlements and later of towns and cities. With its rich agricultural promise, the flat lands of the Boyne Valley were irresistible. From earliest times, we know of the presence of sophisticated human societies here.

The most remarkable is the earliest and the least known. A few miles downstream from Slane, the river makes a U-shaped bend, first to the south and then back north again before resuming its easterly course towards Drogheda. In the area embraced by the U stand the three pre-historic burial sites of Dowth, Knowth and Newgrange, the last of which is the most famous. Magnificently excavated and restored in the 1960s, it is one of the greatest monuments from remote antiquity in northern Europe.

Newgrange is a passage tomb in the form of a great corbelled cairn over 100 metres in diameter. The passage that leads to the burial chamber at the heart of the structure is almost 25 metres long and is aligned to allow the rays of the rising sun on the morning of the winter solstice – and on that morning only – to penetrate fully into the chamber. Clearly, this symbolic moment was chosen by the people who built Newgrange for ritual purposes similar to those of mid-winter festivals throughout Europe. The winter solstice marked the beginning of the returning light from the far southern sky. The Neolithic farmers who built this astonishing structure possessed the skills of astronomical observation, together with the quarrying and transport techniques required to acquire the stones and move them into position. Their mastery of construction is evidenced by the system of guttering they put in place to carry off rainwater from the roof to the periphery of the structure.

Who were these people and what language did they speak? We have absolutely no idea. They were not Celts: the Celts did not reach Ireland for another 2,000 years. Newgrange dates from 2500 BC, contemporaneous with the Egyptian pyramids.

One way and another, the Boyne Valley has been continuously settled ever since. In Celtic times, the nearby Hill of Tara was an important royal site – notionally, although never actually, claiming jurisdiction over the entire island. The Normans settled in significant numbers here, as they did wherever they found good land. Of all their remains, Trim Castle is the most imposing. The Battle of the Boyne, perhaps the most important battle in Irish history, was fought barely two kilometres from Newgrange. There are fine country houses here and a vigorous literary tradition.

The Boyne is also a kind of frontier, marking the passage from the eastern province of Leinster towards the northern province of Ulster. Although the provincial border lies further to the north, you can hear the accents begin to change around here and as you travel north you soon reach the rolling drumlin country, that succession of low hills characteristic of south Ulster which was part of the formidable series of natural defences that protected that province from invasion from the south.

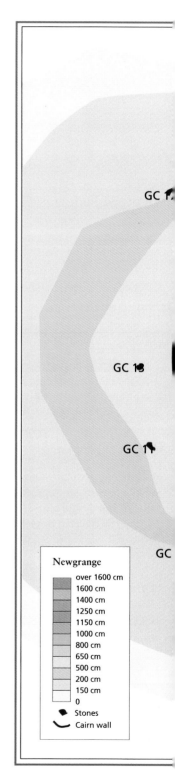

An aerial plan of Newgrange, showing the contours of the mound or cairn with the passage and chamber surrounded by a circle of standing kerb-stones, of which K1 is the magnificently decorated entrance stone. K52, directly opposite it, comes closest to it in terms of the quality of its design and the technique of the decoration. The mound is surrounded by an outer series of undecorated standing stones marked "GC" (after O'Kelly).

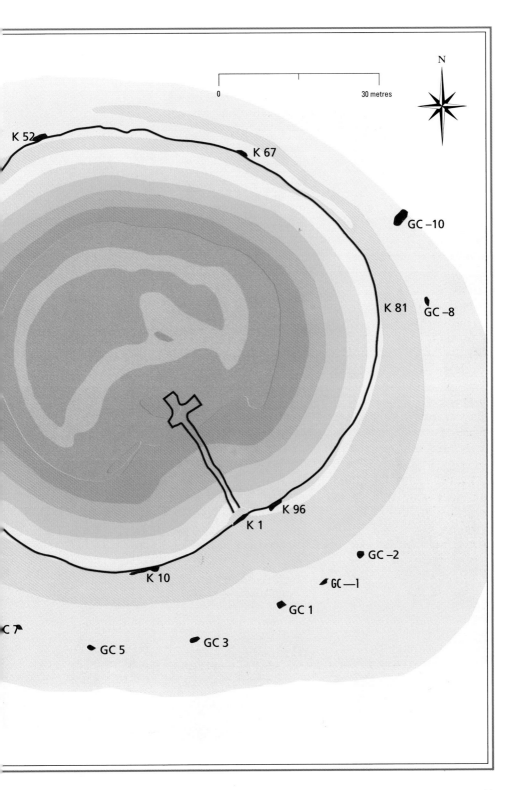

2500 BC

2400 BC
Copper mines in operation at Ross Island, Co. Kerry, among earliest evidence of metal extraction and working in Ireland.

c. 2300 BC
Beginning of Bronze Age.

c. 2200 BC
Early work in beaten gold: bands, discs and lunulae.

Examples of fine quality Bronze Age metalwork, including a copperhead axehead which would have been cast in an open mould and socketed spearheads cast in complex moulds where a plug was used to form the socket.

c. 2000 BC
Pottery vessels: food bowls, beakers, funerary urns.

c. 1000 BC
Increasing sophistication of bronze and gold working: swords, dress fasteners, ornaments etc. Evidence of growing continental influence on insular styles.

c. 500 BC
Emain Macha (Navan fort), Co. Armagh, the centre of Ulaidh power and the supposed palace of King Conchubhar in the Tain Bo Cuailgne, the greatest of the ancient Irish heroic cycles. The Ulaidh people's name survived in the later provincial name Ulaidh/Ulster.

c. 250 BC
Gradual series of incursions by Celtic peoples, who come in successive waves over centuries, until the entire island is finally occupied by Gaelic-speaking Celts early in the Christian era.

c. 250 BC
End of Bronze Age; beginning of Iron Age. Influence of La Tène decorative style from continental Europe.

c. 200 BC
Turoe Stone, Co. Galway, an important early Celtic artefact with decorated carvings in the La Tène style.

c. 150 BC
Broighter Hoard, a unique group of gold objects – including a decorated collar, a boat, a model cauldron and neck chains – excavated at Broighter, Co. Derry, close to Lough Foyle. They are almost certainly of Roman rather than of Irish provenance, an early example of luxury imports.

51 BC
Julius Caesar's *de Bello Gallico*: first written use of the word Hibernia to describe Ireland.

AD 83
The Roman general Gnaeus Julius Agricola defeats the Scots Celts at the battle of Mons Graupius in Aberdeenshire. He then considers an invasion of Ireland, but is recalled to Rome and the plans lapse.

c. 150
Ptolemy's map of Ireland: first recognisable outline of the island.

c. 400
Development of ogham, the oldest surviving form of Irish script comprising a series of horizontal strokes of varying lengths incised on stone or wood: the language was an antique version of Early Irish (Gaelic).

409
Withdrawal of Romans from Britain.

431
Pope Celestine sends Palladius as first bishop to Irish Christians, indicating presence of small Christian community in Ireland prior to arrival of St Patrick.

432
Beginning of St Patrick's mission.

c. 450
Reign of Niall Noígiallach (Niall of the Nine Hostages), ancestral founder of the Uí Néill/O'Neill dynasty.

C. AD 700

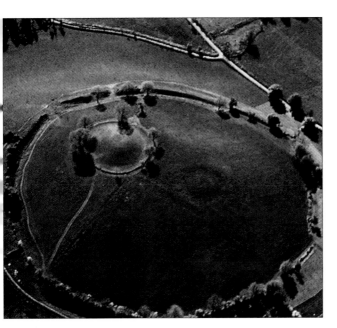

Navan Fort, the ancient Emain Macha in Co. Armagh, 'capital' of Ulster at the dawn of Irish history. This was the ceremonial headquarters of the Ulaid and plays a central part in the early medieval saga literature of Ireland.

461
Death of St Patrick.

516
Battle of Druim Derge establishes Uí Néill power in Irish midlands.

524
Death of St Brigid, abbess of Kildare and one of Ireland's national saints.

546
Foundation of monastery and settlement at Doire Colum Cille (later Derry/Londonderry) by St Colum Cille.

547
Foundation of monastic settlement of Clonmacnoise, the greatest ecclesiastical centre of learning in medieval Ireland, by St Ciaran.

555
Monastery of Bangor founded by St Comgall.

561
Exile of St Colum Cille to Iona.

575
Convention of Druim Cett: St Colum Cille mediates between the Uí Néill and the king of Dalriada.

c. 590
Mission of St Columbanus, greatest of Irish missionaries to the European continent, begins.

597
The Cathach, the oldest surviving Irish manuscript, allegedly composed in the hand of St Colum Cille himself, now in the Royal Irish Academy.

597
Death of St Colum Cille.

597
Arrival of Roman mission of St Augustine to Canterbury, which will have fateful effect on the development of the Celtic church.

610
St Columbanus expelled from Burgundy; removes to St Gall and later to Bobbio, where he dies in 615.

c. 630
Mission of St Fursa to East Anglia.

635
Beginning of St Aidan's mission from Iona to Northumbria, where he founds the monastery of Lindisfarne.

c. 650
Composition of the Book of Durrow, the first major Irish illuminated manuscript.

664
Synod of Whitby resolves long-standing dispute about the date of Easter. The Celtic and Roman churches differed in the method employed to calculate the date. King of Northumbria agrees to accept Roman practice. Iona follows suit in 716.

689
Irish evangelist St Killian martyred at Wurzburg in northern Bavaria.

697
St Adomnan's Vitae Columbae/Life of St Columba (Colum Cille).

c. 700
Composition of the Lindisfarne Gospels.

c. 750

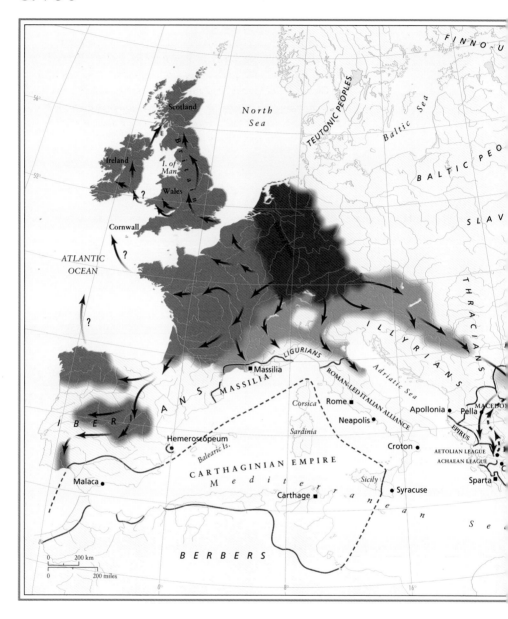

c. 750

Golden Age of insular art: Tara Brooch, Ardagh Chalice, Derrynaflan Chalice etc.

774

Foundation of the abbey of Tallaght near Dublin by Mael Ruain, an important Céile Dé. The Céile

Dé/Culdees were an ascetic reform group within the Irish church, rejecting what they regarded as its excessive worldliness.

795

First Viking raids on Irish coast, at Lambay Island near Dublin.

c. 800

Book of Kells, the most celebrated and beautiful of all insular illuminated manuscripts, now in Trinity College, Dublin. Originally composed in Iona, it was brought to the monastery of Kells, Co. Meath, for safe keeping, following Viking attacks on Iona in 802.

C. 800

The Book of Kells, preserved in Trinity College, Dublin, is a copy of the Gospels written in Latin, most famous for its lavishly decorated full-page depictions of the Four Evangelists and their symbols, portraits of the Virgin and Child and of Christ, including the depiction of His temptation and arrest, as seen in the accompanying photograph. However, even the text pages are full of life, the initial letters being decorated with often comical human and animal figures.

*I*n the second half of the first millennium BC, during what prehistorians call the Iron Age, the first Celtic peoples began to arrive in Ireland, though there is no surviving evidence of a large-scale invasion. The people known to the Greeks as Keltoi or Celts had dominated central and western Europe and spoke an Indo-European language which developed into P-Celtic, the language of Britain and Gaul, ancestor of Welsh and Breton, and Q-Celtic, the language of the Celtic inhabitants of Ireland, ancestor of Gaelic.

Celtic culture of this period is called La Tène after a site in Switzerland, and objects in the La Tène style survive mainly from the north and west of Ireland.

Christian Missionaries

O NE OF THE hoariest shibboleths in Irish history is the one about the country never being part of the Roman Empire. Well, yes and no. Certainly, in a formal sense Ireland was never a province of Rome like England, Wales and southern Scotland. But there were vigorous trading links between Roman Britain and Ireland, not to mention Irish seaborne raids on wealthy Roman settlements.

When the Roman empire finally came to Ireland in the fifth century AD, it did so in spiritual rather than in military form. Christianity had been adopted as the official religion of the empire two centuries earlier, at the time of Constantine. So the Christianisation of Ireland was also a form of Romanisation.

That said, early Irish Christianity differed significantly from the orthodox Roman system of church government. Roman church government was based on the diocesan model, which was basically territorial. The early Irish church, however, preferred a monastic model in which kinship ties were more important than territorial ones. This reflected the dynastic and tribal nature of Gaelic society. Indeed, there appears to have been a pattern of locating the new Christian churches and monasteries close to pre-existing centres of secular power. Likewise, the early Christians absorbed many of the Celtic pagan feasts and usages, adapting them to the requirements of the new religion.

St Patrick, the national apostle, was a Romanised Briton who first came to Ireland in AD 432. He was not the first Christian evangelist in the island but he was the most important and the one whose legacy was the most enduring. Within two centuries of his mission, the entire island had been thoroughly Christianised, with monasteries and churches in every district. Moreover, the bigger monasteries had developed into proto-universities, centres not only of piety and contemplation but of scholarship and learning. This was important, because it occurred contemporaneously with the period in continental history known as the Dark Ages. Following the final collapse of the Roman Empire, the civic order that the empire had ordained and underwritten was subverted by the relentless incursions of wave after wave of nomadic and destructive tribes. They came from the Asian steppes, across the Northern European plain that lay outside the border of the empire and progressively occupied imperial territory. The two principal ethnic groups were the Germans and the Slavs.

The fifth century brought the collapse of the old imperial system. Rome itself was sacked by the Visigoths in 410 and by the Vandals in 455. The Roman Empire in the west ended in 476 and thereafter Italy was dominated by Ostrogoths and Lombards. In theory, the imperial capital moved eastwards to Byzantium (modern Istanbul), with Italy a province of the empire. In practice, this was a fiction. The one remaining link with the old system was the

Pope, still resident in Rome but increasingly dependant on the military support of Christian kings beyond Italy, of whom Charlemagne was to be the most significant.

Gradually, the Christianisation of the Germanic and Slav tribes began. This meant the re-establishment of an imperial uniformity in spiritual matters not only within the boundaries of the old empire but beyond. It was a tremendous enterprise. In all, it spread Chritianity across the entire continent – Lithuania was the last territory to accept papal authority, but not until 1385 – and as far afield as Syria. By the time it was complete, the Christian world was hopelessly divided between the Latin and Orthodox churches, reflecting the old division between Greek Byzantium and Latin Rome.

The Irish contribution to this enormous millennial movement was critical. It was focused on the golden age of Irish Christianity, from AD 600 to 800, although Irish influence persisted long thereafter. In that central period, the principal evangelists were St Colum Cille, who established the faith in northwestern Britain, and his successor St Aidan, who spread it to Northumbria, founding the famous religious house at Lindisfarne; St Fursa, who evangelised East Anglia and parts of northern France; and most important of all, St Columbanus, whose foundations in central Europe made him, along with St Benedict, a seminal figure in the European monastic tradition.

Ireland's remoteness had preserved it from the upheavals on the continent at the end of the imperial era. The Christian church had established itself and thrived. The missionaries of the golden age were carrying back to the shattered lands of the old empire the faith which they had embraced from it in its dying days. Once the old imperial lands were again secure for Christianity, there then began the vast push north and east that ended in Lithuania at the end of the fourteenth century. There was Irish influence here too – we know of Irish missionaries as far east as Kiev in medieval times – but the key contribution had been made earlier.

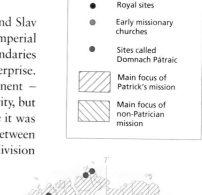

The Arrival of Christianity

- Royal sites
- Early missionary churches
- Sites called Domnach Pátraic
- Main focus of Patrick's mission
- Main focus of non-Patrician mission

Downpatrick
Emain Macha
Armagh (St Patrick)
Saul
Cruachu
Tara
Dunshaughlin (St Secundinus)
Kilashee (St Auxilius)
Naas
Kilcullen
Dún Ailinne
Seir Kieran (St Ciarán)
Sletty
Emly (St Ailbe)
Cashel
Ardmore (St Declan)

(1) St Patrick from Britain, mid-5th century

(2) St Secundinus from continent, mid-5th century ?

(3) St Auxilius from continent, mid-5th century ?

(4) St Iserninus from continent, mid-5th century ?

(5) Early Gaulish and British missionary activity, late 4th – early 5th centuries

(6) Palladius from Auxerre (?), AD 431

17

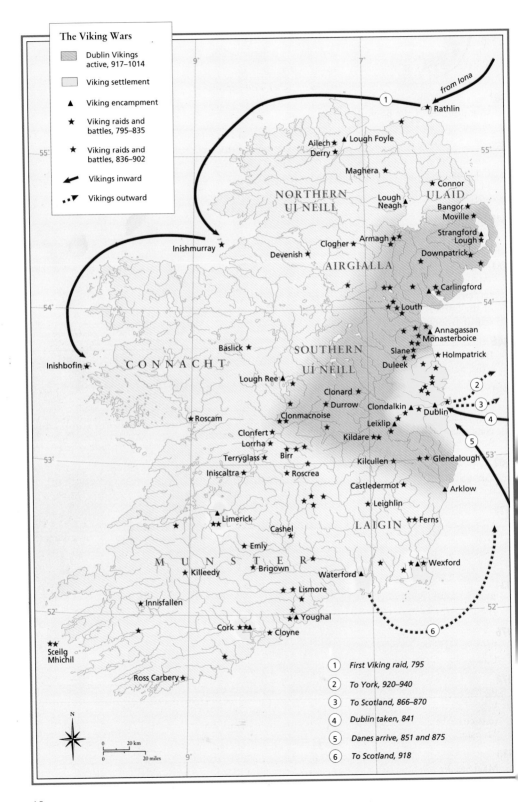

The Viking Wars

Dublin Vikings active, 917–1014

Viking settlement

▲ Viking encampment

★ Viking raids and battles, 795–835

★ Viking raids and battles, 836–902

→ Vikings inward

⋯▶ Vikings outward

from Iona

① Rathlin

Ailech ★   ▲ Lough Foyle
Derry ★

Maghera ★

NORTHERN
UÍ NÉILL

Lough Neagh ▲

ULAID

★ Connor

Bangor ★ ★
Moville ★

Strangford ▲
Lough ★

Downpatrick ★
★

Inishmurray ★

Clogher ★   Armagh ★ ★

Devenish ★

AIRGIALLA

★

★ ★   ★ ▲ Carlingford

★ ★ Louth
★

★ ★ ▲ Annagassan
Monasterboice

Baslick ★

SOUTHERN
UÍ NÉILL

Slane ★
Duleek ★

★ Holmpatrick
★

Lough Ree ▲ ★

Clonard ★

Durrow ★   Clondalkin ▲ ▲
★ ★ Dublin

Roscam ★

Clonmacnoise
★ ★

Leixlip ▲

Clonfert ★
Lorrha ★

Kildare ★ ★

②

③

④

Terryglass ★   Birr
Iniscaltra ★   ★ Roscrea

Kilcullen ★

★ ★ Glendalough

⑤

Castledermot ★

★ ★ ★

★ Leighlin

▲ Arklow

★ Limerick
★ ★

Cashel
★

Emly ★

LAIGIN

★ ★ Ferns

M U N S T E R ★
★ Killeedy   ★ Brigown

Waterford ▲

★   ★ ★ ★ Wexford

★ Innisfallen

★ ★ Lismore

Cork ★ ★ ▲   ★ Cloyne

★ ▲ Youghal

★ ★
Sceilg
Mhichíl

★

⑥

Ross Carbery ★

N

0   20 km
0   20 miles

① First Viking raid, 795
② To York, 920–940
③ To Scotland, 866–870
④ Dublin taken, 841
⑤ Danes arrive, 851 and 875
⑥ To Scotland, 918

1134

c. 800
Continuing and devastating Viking raids on monastic sites.

807
Composition of the Book of Armagh.

820
Primacy of Feidlimid mac Crimthainn, king of Munster in southern half of Ireland.

840
Feidlimid mac Crimthainn occupies Tara.

841
Vikings establish trading settlement near the mouth of the Liffey; origin of the city of Dublin.

846
Death of Feidlimid mac Crimthainn.

863
Vikings plunder Newgrange and other Neolithic burial sites in the Boyne Valley.

902
Vikings abandon Dublin, but return in 925.

922
Vikings establish settlement at head of Shannon Estuary: origin of the city of Limerick.

934
Rise of the sub-kingdom of Dal Cais in west Munster.

976
Brian Boru king of Dal Cais.

978
Brian Boru wins Battle of Belach Lechta (Co. Cork) to become king of Munster.

980
Mael Seachnaill, king of southern Uí Néill, claims high kingship of Ireland.

981
Mael Seachnaill captures Dublin.

997
Ireland divided in two between Mael Seachnaill and Brian Boru.

999
Battle of Glen Máma near Dublin: Brian Boru defeats coalition of Mael Seachnaill and Dublin Vikings.

1000
Brian Boru captures Dublin.

1002
Brian Boru high king of Ireland.

1005
Brian Boru confirms the primacy of the see of Armagh in the Irish church.

1014
Revolt against Brian Boru leads to Battle of Clontarf near Dublin. The king of Leinster, aided by Vikings from the Orkneys and the Isle of Man, are defeated by Brian. However, Brian is killed towards the end of the battle. Mael Seachnaill claims high kingship following Brian's death, but neither he nor his successors could establish an undisputed claim. Brian's death was the last chance to create a united Gaelic kingdom in Ireland.

c. 1028
Consecration of Dúnán/Donatus, the first known bishop of Dublin, possibly at Canterbury.

c. 1030
Foundation of Christ Church cathedral, Dublin.

1066
Norman conquest of England.

1074
Consecration at Canterbury of Gilla Pádraic/Patricius as bishop of Dublin. He was the first bishop of Dublin definitely to be consecrated there, emphasising Canterbury's primatial claim over the see of Dublin.

1092
Beginning of composition of the Annals of Innisfallen, the earliest surviving annalistic manuscript.

1096
First known bishop of Waterford consecrated at Canterbury.

1097
Burning of the round tower at Monasterboice, Co. Louth, containing the monastery's library and other treasures.

1111
Synod of Ráith Bressail advances church reform, establishes two archbishoprics in Armagh and Cashel.

1122
Ua Conchobair/O'Connor dynasty of Connacht displace Ua Briain/O'Briens of Munster as "high kings with opposition".

1124
Completion of the round tower at Clonmacnoise.

1134
Consecration of Cormac's Chapel on the Rock of Cashel, one of the most important buildings of the Irish Romanesque period.

1142

1142

Foundation by St Malachy of Armagh of first Irish Cistercian abbey at Mellifont, Co. Louth.

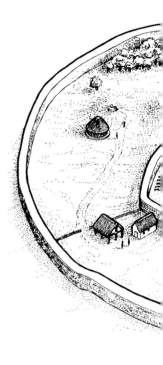

1152

Synod of Kells establishes four ecclesiastical provinces in Ireland, adding Dublin and Tuam to the pre-existing Armagh and Cashel. It also confirmed other reforms in the Irish church, which received papal approval. The establishment of Dublin as a province within the Irish church meant the tacit rejection of Canterbury's primatial claim over the Dublin diocese.

1155

The papal bull Laudabiliter issued by Pope Adrian IV (Nicholas Breakspear, the only English pope) authorises King Henry II of England to invade Ireland in order to effect further ecclesiastical reform. The authenticity of the bull has been disputed. It is highly probable that the motivation for the issue of the bull lay with the see of Canterbury, resenting its loss of influence in Ireland under the provisions of the Synod of Kells.

1162

Synod of Clane re-asserts primacy of Armagh in Irish church.

1162

Lorcán Ua Tuathail/Lorcan O'Toole archbishop of Dublin: consecrated by archbishop of Armagh.

Ireland Before the Normans, c. 1100	
MIDE	Over-kingdoms
Airthir	Sub-kingdoms and territories
UA NÉILL	Principal dynastic surnames
Ua Bric	Lesser dynastic surnames
🏰	Trading city or town

1169

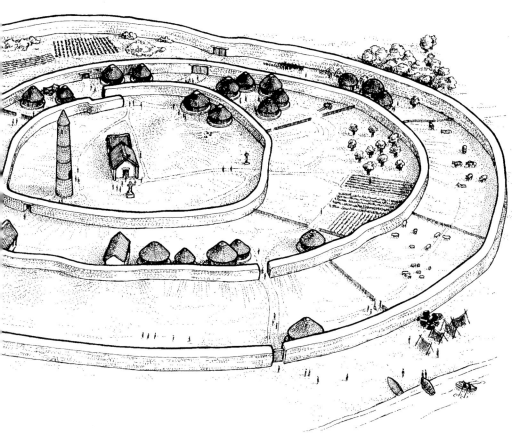

1166
Ruaidrí Ua Conchobair/Rory O'Connor, king of Connacht since 1156, becomes high king with opposition.

1166
Diarmait Mac Murchada/Dermot MacMurrough deposed as king of Leinster following long-running dispute with Tigernán Ua Ruairc/Tiernan O'Rourke, king of Breiffne which ends with the destruction of Mac Murchada's stronghold at Ferns, Co. Wexford. Mac Murchada, who had also unsuccessfully challenged Ruaidrí Ua Conchobair for the high kingship, is exiled by the latter.

1167
Mac Murchada offers fealty to King Henry II and is allowed to recruit among Norman knights in Wales. He returns to Ireland with a small party of Normans and recovers his ancestral lands, but not all of Leinster.

1169
Larger party of Normans lands at Bannow Bay, Co. Wexford, the first of a series of Norman landings in support of Mac Murchada.

The early Christian monastery of Nendrum is located on Mahee Island in Strangford Lough, Co. Down, and is only accessible by causeway. It was founded perhaps as early as the 5th century by St Mochaoi and excavations have shown that its various quarters were divided by a series of three concentric walls, the first wall surrounding the monastery buildings themselves, including a small stone church and the stump of a Round Tower dating from the 10th or 11th century. Within the other walls stood more buildings, including workshops and perhaps a school (after Hamlin).

MEDIEVAL IRELAND

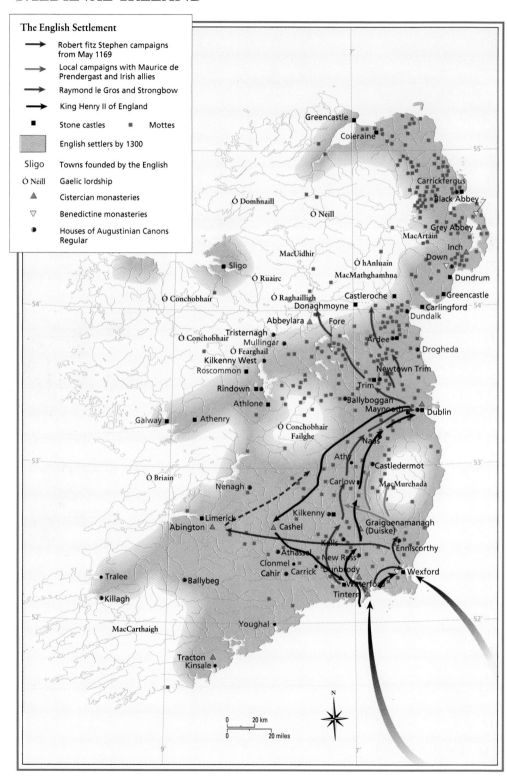

The English Settlement

→ Robert fitz Stephen campaigns from May 1169

→ Local campaigns with Maurice de Prendergast and Irish allies

→ Raymond le Gros and Strongbow

→ King Henry II of England

■ Stone castles ■ Mottes

English settlers by 1300

Sligo Towns founded by the English

Ó Néill Gaelic lordship

▲ Cistercian monasteries

▽ Benedictine monasteries

◗ Houses of Augustinian Canons Regular

Greencastle
Coleraine
Carrickfergus
Black Abbey
Grey Abbey
Ó Domhnaill
Ó Néill
MacArtain
Inch
Down
Ó hAnluain
MacUidhir
Sligo
Ó Ruairc
MacMathghamhna
Dundrum
Ó Conchobhair
Ó Raghailligh
Castleroche
Greencastle
Donaghmoyne
Carlingford
Abbeylara
Fore
Dundalk
Tristernagh
Ó Conchobhair
Ardee
Mullingar
Drogheda
Ó Fearghail
Kilkenny West
Newtown Trim
Roscommon
Trim
Rindown
Newtown Trim
Athlone
Ballyboggan
Galway
Athenry
Maynooth
Dublin
Ó Conchobhair
Failghe
Naas
Athy
Ó Briain
Castledermot
Nenagh
Carlow
MacMurchada
Kilkenny
Graiguenamanagh
(Duiske)
Limerick
Ennlscorthy
Abington
Cashel
Kells
Athassel
New Ross
Wexford
Tralee
Clonmel
Dunbrody
Cahir
Carrick
Waterford
Ballybeg
Tintern
Killagh
MacCarthaigh
Youghal
Tracton
Kinsale

N

0   20 km

0   20 miles

1197

1170

Arrival of other leading Norman knights, including Raymond le Gros fitz William and Richard fitz Gilbert, deposed earl of Pembroke – better known as Strongbow. They capture Waterford; Strongbow marries Aoife, daughter of Diarmait Mac Murchada.

1170

Dublin falls to Mac Murchada and his Norman allies. They make further incursions in Leinster and Meath.

1171

Death of Diarmait Mac Murchada, who is succeeded as king of Leinster by Strongbow.

1171

Both the deposed Norse king of Dublin, Askulv, and the high king, Ruaidrí Ua Conchobair, are unsuccessful in their efforts to re-capture the city from the Normans by siege.

1171

King Henry II, fearing that Strongbow might establish an independent kingship, comes to Ireland to assert his authority. Strongbow submits and is granted the kingdom of Leinster as Henry's vassal. A number of Gaelic kings also submit to Henry.

1171

King Henry grants a charter to the city of Dublin.

1172

Hugh de Lacy granted Meath, formerly the heartland of the southern Uí Néill.

1174

Defeats for Normans in Meath and Tipperary.

1175

Treaty of Windsor between Henry II and Ruaidrí Ua Conchobair asserts Henry's lordship over Leinster and Meath.

1176

Death of Strongbow.

1177

John de Courcy invades and occupies eastern Ulster.

1177

Prince John, son of Henry II, officially proclaimed Lord of Ireland.

1180

John de Courcy marries the daughter of King of Man; Hugh de Lacy marries the daughter of the high king Ruaidrí.

c. 1180

de Courcy begins construction of Carrickfergus Castle, the most impressive Norman fortified site in Ulster.

1183

Abdication of Ruaidrí Ua Conchobair in favour of his son.

1185

Arrival of Prince John, Lord of Ireland, at Waterford. He is accompanied by Theobald Walter, his butler, founder of the Butler family of Ormond.

1186

Hugh de Lacy murdered.

1189

Death of Henry II, succeeded by Richard I (the Lionheart).

1190

Foundation of St Patrick's cathedral, Dublin, by archbishop John Comyn.

1197

Charter for the city of Limerick.

The seal of Richard fitz Gilbert de Clare, lord of Pembroke, alias Strongbow, the Norman marcher lord and leader of a group of Norman warrior lords based in the Welsh border lands. He arrived in August 1170, allied to Diarmait Mac Murchada. He quickly took the Viking city of Waterford. Strongbow received his reward by marrying Mac Murchada's daughter, Aoife. Diarmait's death in May 1171, without legitimate male heirs, meant that his kingdom of Leinster came into Strongbow's possession through Aoife.

23

1199

1199
Prince John, Lord of Ireland, succeeds to English throne on the death of his brother Richard.

1199
Dublin the first Irish county to be shired.

c. 1200
Establishment of the Irish exchequer.

1202
Cathal Crobderg Ua Conchobair established as king of Connacht with support of the de Burgo/Burke family.

1204
First instructions issued by King John to build a royal castle in Dublin.

1204
Construction begins on Kilkenny Castle.

1207
Arrival in Ireland of William Marshall, the most powerful magnate in either island, to oversee his possessions, which include the kingdom of Leinster. He endows Cistercian abbey at Graiguenamanagh (Duiske).

1207
Shiring of Cork and Waterford.

1210
King John lands at Waterford. He imposes royal authority on Norman lords and confirms that Irish law shall be the same as English law.

1215
Geoffrey de Marisco appointed justiciar for the first of three terms of office.

1217
Establishment of the Irish Treasury.

1218
First itinerant justices to administer the Common Law in those parts of Ireland under royal control.

1219
Death of John de Courcy.

1219
Death of William Marshall the elder, earl of Pembroke and lord of Leinster, the most influential of the Norman lords in Ireland at the time of his death.

1220
Rebuilding of Trim Castle, Co. Meath.

c. 1223
Construction begins on Kildare cathedral, on the site of St Brigid's fifth-century monastery.

1224
Arrival of the Dominican order in Ireland.

1227
Kingdom of Connacht, except for five eastern cantreds reserved for the king, granted to Richard de Burgo/Burke, who fights series of local wars to establish his claim.

1231
Establishment of first Franciscan friaries in Ireland.

1231
Death of William Marshall the younger.

1232
Establishment of the Irish Chancery.

1232
Foundation of Norman castle at Galway, the origin of the town that later developed around it.

1234
Richard de Burgo confirmed as king of Connacht.

1235
Charter granted by Richard de Burgo to Meiler de Bermingham results in development of Athenry, Co. Galway, an important civil and religious stronghold in east Connacht.

1236
Foundation of castle at Loughrea, Co. Galway.

1240
King Henry III announces planned expedition to Ireland for following year: it never takes place.

1243
Death of Hugh de Lacy without male successor ends direct line and sees earldom of Ulster revert to the crown.

1245
Deaths of brothers Walter and Anselm Marshall, ending the male line: inheritance is split between five heiresses.

1248
Foundation of Bunratty Castle, Co. Clare.

1248

Carrickfergus, which means 'the Rock of Fergus', was a fortress since early historic times, the rock in question providing strategic access to Belfast Lough. Little wonder, then, that Ulster's larger-than-life conqueror, John de Courcy, should select it for the site of a castle of his own soon after 1177, and that it emerged as the principal town of Anglo-Norman Ulster.

The castle drawn in black was completed by 1200, later additions in red by 1225 and in blue by 1250 (after McNeill).

Norman Ireland

A galloglass (gall-óglach, "foreign warrior"), imported from the west of Scotland. These heavily armoured and well-equipped fighters effected the balance of power.

GAELIC IRELAND was a cultural unity. The Gaels were a Celtic people who had conquered the entire island around 400 BC. For over a thousand years, they lived in insular isolation. They raided and traded with Britain and parts of the continent but they were undisturbed by the outside world. The cultural integrity of Gaelic Ireland – its common systems of law and language – even absorbed and survived the introduction of the alien Christian religion.

This integral world enjoyed its golden age in the early, heroic centuries of Christian missionary endeavour, from AD 600 to 800. The Irish monasteries were centres not just of learning but of wealth. And it was this wealth that first attracted the attention of predatory outsiders. In 795, the Vikings appeared off the Irish coast, raiding and plundering the poorly defended monasteries. These ferocious warriors, the greatest navigators of the age, were also traders and settlers. Most Irish cities, including Dublin, began as Viking trading settlements.

Viking settlement from 800 to 1100 meant a series of shifting alliances with the perennially fractious Gaelic dynasties. There developed a rough and ready co-existence between the Viking settlements and the Gaelic kingdoms. Attempts by Brian Boru – originally a small provincial sub-king – to create a united Irish kingdom in the early eleventh century by military conquest failed. Thereafter, no single ruler could command the allegiance of the entire island.

Into this culturally homogeneous but politically fractured world, the arrival of the Normans in the late 1160s was a revolutionary event. The Normans were descendants of Viking raiders who had settled in northern France some centuries earlier. They were a part of the huge wave of colonisation from the Frankish lands – roughly northern France and western Germany. The Franks pushed into eastern Germany and Poland; south as far as Sicily, which was conquered by the Normans; and, at the end of the eleventh century, as far as Palestine where they established the Crusader kingdoms.

The Norman invasion of England in 1066 was part of this thrust. The capture of the relatively centralised English royal system meant the capture of the kingdom itself. In Scotland, the Norman incursion in the lowlands happened by royal invitation, as the kings of Scotland needed the help of the new power to the south in their constant struggle to maintain the unity of the kingdom.

The Normans displayed no immediate interest in Ireland, nor did anyone in Ireland show much interest in them. But in 1166, the king of Leinster, Diarmaid MacMurrough, was ousted following a dynastic row. He solicited help from King Henry II of England, who eventually approved his raising an invasion party among the Norman knights of Wales. The first Normans landed in Co. Wexford in 1169 and their superior military technology made itself felt immediately.

The similarity between Ireland and Scotland was that the Normans had come to both countries by invitation. The difference was that whereas in Scotland they were invited to bolster the forces of a more-or-less centralised kingdom, in Ireland they were enlisted in an internecine fight. They quickly imposed themselves, capturing the key towns of Waterford and Dublin. Indeed, so successful were they that the king – whose principal interests lay in England and western France and for whom Ireland was distraction – was obliged to take control. In 1171, Henry came to Dublin to accept the submission of both its new Norman rulers and of many leading Gaelic princes.

The latter did not include Rory O'Connor, the latest disputed claimant to the title of high king of Ireland but certainly the strongest individual Gaelic king. It may be doubted that Henry and the Gaelic kings understood this submission to mean the same thing: the whole structure of European feudalism which was essential to the Norman understanding of legal obligation was unknown in Gaelic Ireland. Henry now regarded the Gaelic kings who had submitted as his liegemen; they probably understood a tactical and provisional retreat in the Gaelic manner.

A formal arrangement between Henry and Rory was reached in the so-called Treaty of Windsor in 1175: Henry claimed lordship over the kingdoms of Leinster and Meath including the towns of Dublin, Wexford and Waterford; Rory was confirmed as king of Connacht and overlord of the areas not claimed by Henry, but subject to a tribute payable to Henry. The fluid circumstances on the ground in Ireland made the treaty impossible to enforce. There was simply too much juggling for position among the new Norman landowners struggling to stake their claims, while the dynastic disputes between the Gaelic kings continued. Indeed, the Norman incursions became part of the traditional dynamic. As with the Vikings, there were alliances across ethnic lines: it was not a simple matter of Norman versus Gael. For instance, Rory O'Connor married his daughter to Hugh de Lacy, the greatest of the new Norman lords.

This fateful and confused series of events marks the first direct involvement of the English crown in Ireland: the claim to the lordship of Ireland dates from 1177, when Henry granted the title to his son John. Henceforth, the kings of England regarded themselves as overlords of all Ireland, with good legal title to the claim.

1251

1251
First Irish mint opened at Dublin.

1251
Construction begins at St Canice's cathedral, Kilkenny.

1252
John fitz Thomas FitzGerald defeats Gaelic king of Desmond at battle of Baile Uí Dúnadaig in east Cork: first significant incursion of Fitzgerald power into Desmond.

The Anglo-Irish victory at the Battle of Athenry in 1316 is commemorated in the seal of the town. The severed heads may represent the vanquished chieftains of Connacht. Five Irish kings are said to have died in this battle.

1258
Attempted revival of high kingship: O'Connors of Connacht, O'Briens of Thomond and O'Neills of Tyrone agree on Brian O'Neill as high king.

1259
Aed O'Connor, son of the king of Connacht, marries a daughter of Dougal MacSorley of the Western Isles in Scotland and receives a dowry including 160 galloglass mercenaries, the first appearance in Ireland of these feared troops.

1260
Death of Brian O'Neill at battle of Downpatrick. His head sent to London.

1262
Gaelic kings offer high kingship to King Haakon IV of Norway if he will agree to help them drive the English from Ireland.

1264
First meeting of an Irish parliament, at Castledermot, Co. Kildare.

c. 1270
First Irish Carmelite friary established, at Leighlinbridge, Co. Carlow.

c. 1280
Consecration of St Canice's cathedral, Kilkenny.

1297
Parliament in Dublin forbids wearing of Gaelic dress by members of the English colony, evidence of gradual gaelicisation.

1310
Parliament meeting at Kilkenny passes statute forbidding membership of English religious houses to Irish men.

1311
Ongoing military pressure on the Dublin area from Gaelic resurgence: O'Byrnes and O'Tooles from the Wicklow highlands destroy outlying settlements of Saggart and Rathcoole.

1315
Invasion of Ireland by Edward Bruce. He lands at Larne, captures Dundalk and defeats the earl of Ulster.

1315
Beginning of three years of famine in western Europe, including Ireland.

1316
Edward Bruce crowned king of Ireland, captures Carrickfergus Castle. Robert Bruce, king of Scotland, lands in Ireland.

1316
John fitz Thomas Fitzgerald first earl of Kildare.

1317
Edward and Robert encamp near Dublin, but pull back north as English reinforcements under Mortimer land at Youghal and push towards Dublin. Robert Bruce returns to Dublin.

1318
Battle of Faughart: defeat and death of Edward Bruce.

1318
Battle of Dysert O'Dea: Gaelic king of Thomond defeats his Anglo-Norman overlord, Richard de Clare, thus preventing the establishment of an English lordship in what later became Co. Clare.

1320
First stone bridge across the River Barrow built at Leighlinbridge by Maurice Jakis, canon of Kildare cathedral.

1320
Dublin parliament approves

Irish Dynasties and
English Settlement, *c.* 1300

Counties and liberties

Irish chiefdoms

Allegiance of Irish chiefdoms

● The King of England

● The Earl of Ulster

● The Lord of Connacht

● The Lord of Trim

● The Lord of Thomond

*The Lordship of Meath was
partitioned in 1244 into two
estates, one administered
from Trim, the other from Kells*

U l s t e r

O'Donnell

O'Neill

Carrickfergus

Lough
Neagh

MacCartan

Downpatrick
*Down
1260*

Maguire

O'Connor
of Sligo

O'Rourke

O'Hanlon

MacMahon

Louth

O'Reilly

C o n n a c h t

O'Connor

Meath

Kells

Drogheda

Roscommon

O'Farrell

T r i m

Trim

Meath

Dublin

Galway

Athenry

O'Connor
Faly

K i l d a r e

Dublin

O'Brien

T h o m o n d

Kilkenny

Carlow

to Kildare

MacMurrough

Limerick

T i p p e r a r y

Kilkenny

Limerick

Cashel

W e x f o r d

K e r r y

Waterford

Wexford

Wexford

W a t e r f o r d

C o r k

MacCarthy

Cork

N

0   20 km

0   20 miles

1321

This carving, from St Mary's Church at Gowran, Co. Kilkenny, is believed to be of the first Countess of Ormond, whose husband James Butler (d. 1338) was head of one of the premier families of Anglo-Norman descent in Ireland. They derived their surname from the fact that the first of their Anglo-Irish ancestors, Theobald Walter, was butler in the household of Prince John when he came to Ireland in 1185 and was granted extensive estates in north Munster and later in Leinster.

the establishment of an Irish university, but nothing comes of the decision.

1321
Envoys from Cistercian mother house in Clairvaux arrive in Ireland to end practice of discriminating against Irish entrants to Cistercian houses in Ireland.

1324
Dame Alice Kyteler of Kilkenny convicted on charges of witchcraft laid by Richard Ledrede, the Franciscan bishop of Ossory. The most famous of the Irish witchcraft trials, it was part of a local power struggle among her family and the local elite. Dame Alice escaped death, fleeing to England, but her maid, Petronilla de Midia, was burned at the stake.

1328
James Butler created first earl of Ormond.

1329
Maurice fitz Thomas FitzGerald created first earl of Desmond.

1329
Richard Ledrede flees Ireland.

1331
Irish forces capture Tallaght (near Dublin), Arklow and Ferns.

1332
King Edward III plans expedition to Ireland, but is instead preoccupied by situation in Scotland and France.

1348
First appearance of the Black Death in Ireland.

1351
Great council at Kilkenny passes legislation similar in wording and intent to later

Statute of Kilkenny (1366).

1360
Delegates appointed by Council at Kilkenny to petition the king regarding dangers to the colony caused by the resurgence of the Gaelic Irish.

1361
Lionel of Clarence, third son of Edward III and husband of the heiress to the earldom of Ulster, sent to Ireland in new role of lieutenant.

1366
Statute of Kilkenny, the most complete attempt by parliament to arrest the growing gaelicisation of the Anglo-Norman colony. It prescribes the exclusive use of the English language, the Common Law and English forms of nomenclature. It attempts to proscribe Irish forms of dress and horsemanship as well as inter-marriage and fosterage between the races.

1369
William of Windsor appointed king's lieutenant in Ireland.

1375
Art Mac Murrough succeeds to revived Gaelic kingdom of Leinster.

1375
Cahir, Co. Tipperary, passes into the control of the earls of Ormond, who begin the rebuilding of the castle.

1375
Niall O'Neill of Tyrone defeats Anglo-Irish at the battle of Downpatrick, reducing the earldom of Ulster to a rump around Carrickfergus Castle, restoring the ancient power

1462

of Uí Néill/O'Neill and extending it east of the Bann.

1385

Parliament in session in Dublin petitions King Richard II to come to Ireland in person to crush Gaelic Irish revival.

1392

Art Mac Murrough extracts tribute from town of Castledermot.

1394

Arrival of King Richard II at Waterford, with an army of 5,000 – the largest military force seen in medieval Ireland. Art Mac Murrough, king of Leinster, submits to him.

1395

Submission of several Irish kings to Richard II.

1396

Continuing rebellion and unrest, especially in Leinster.

1397

Projected royal expedition to Ireland cancelled.

1398

Death of Gerald FitzGerald, third earl of Desmond known as Gearóid Iarla/Gerald the Earl, the most celebrated Irish-language poet of Norman stock in medieval Ireland.

1398

Roger Mortimer, fourth earl of March and lieutenant of Ireland, killed in battle at Callan, Co. Kilkenny by O'Byrnes and O'Tooles.

1399

Richard II returns to Ireland to renew campaign against Art Mac Murrough, but is forced to return to England to deal

with Bolingbroke rebellion. However, he is deposed by the usurper, who assumes the crown as Henry IV.

1401

Owain Glendower, Welsh rebel, appeals for Irish assistance.

1401

Thomas, duke of Lancaster, appointed royal lieutenant in Ireland.

1403

Border disputes between earls of Ormond and Desmond.

1405

Art Mac Murrough campaigns in south Leinster; his ally O'Byrne destroys settlement of Newcastle, Co. Wicklow.

1408

The lieutenant Lancaster arrests the earl of Kildare and is later wounded in an Irish attack near Dublin.

1412

Town of Galway severely damaged by fire.

1414

Arrival of Sir John Talbot as chief governor.

1416

Death of Art Mac Murrough.

1419

Donnchada Mac Murrough, king of Leinster, captured by Sir John Talbot.

c. 1420

Continuing pressure on the Anglo-Norman colony by the resurgent Gaelic Irish.

1422

Town of Youghal and surrounding region, previously part of the earldom of Ormond, passes into Desmond

control as part of a marriage settlement.

1423

Niall Garbh O'Donnell builds a castle at Ballyshannon, Co. Donegal, commanding the headwaters of the River Erne, one of the most important strategic sites in south-west Ulster: it will remain in Gaelic hands until the early seventeenth century.

1446

Earliest use of the term "Pale" to describe the English-dominated "land of Peace" in the lowland counties around Dublin, marking it off from the marcher "lands of war" beyond.

1449

Richard, duke of York, in Ireland: accepts submission of various Gaelic provincial kings.

c. 1455

Construction of main parts of Holycross Abbey, Co. Tipperary.

1460

Parliament meeting at Drogheda declares that only legislation approved by the Irish parliament should have the force of law in Ireland: the most trenchant statement of colonial autonomy by a medieval Irish parliament.

1461

The Yorkist Edward IV become king of England; appoints Thomas, seventh earl of Kildare, as justiciar.

1462

Battle of Piltown: eighth earl of Desmond defeats his rival Ormond in a contest that echoed the English rivalries of the wars of the Roses.

1465

1465
Parliament meeting at Trim passes act to establish a university at Drogheda.

1468
Parliament at Drogheda. Earls of Desmond and Kildare both attainted; Desmond executed, prompting his brother Gerald to invade Leinster.

1469
King Edward IV a prisoner.

1470
Brief restoration of King Henry VI.

1471
King Edward IV restored to throne following defeat of Henry VI at Battle of Tewkesbury. Earl of Kildare appointed lord deputy.

1487
Lambert Simnel, Yorkist imposter, is crowned king of England in Dublin. His claim is quickly snuffed out.

1488
Anglo-Irish supporters of Lambert Simnel pardoned by king. Kildare confirmed in office.

1491
Perkin Warbeck, another Yorkist pretender, lands at Cork.

1491
Kildare dismissed as deputy.

1494
Edward Poynings appointed deputy. Parliament at Drogheda

1499
Execution of Perkin Warbeck.

1501
Scots defeats by the O'Neills near Armagh.

1504
Battle of Knockdoe: Kildare defeats Ulick Burke of Clanrickard in major encounter.

1505
O'Donnells invade O'Neill heartland in Tyrone, recover Castlederg.

1506
Turlough Donn O'Brien of Thomond bridges River Shannon north of Limerick at site still known as O'Brien's Bridge.

St Patrick's Cathedral, Dublin, 1793, by James Malton. The cathedral is shown here from the south-east and it is a valuable historical document as it shows a fine example of Early Gothic architecture in Ireland before the 19th-century restorations. St Patrick's pre-dated the English invasion, but the extant building was erected after it, and elevated to cathedral status c. 1220.

1478
Death of earl of Kildare. Gearóid Mór (the Great Earl) succeeds to title as eighth earl and to the lord deputyship.

1485
Battle of Bosworth brings Henry VII to the English throne, inaugurating the Tudor dynasty. Earl of Kildare confirmed as lord deputy.

passes "Poynings' Law" designed to limit the freedom of action of the lord deputy, later used to assert the authority of the English parliament over the Irish.

1495
Earl of Kildare arrested.

1496
Kildare restored as deputy.

1509
Death of Henry VII; succeeded by Henry VIII.

1509
Kildare despoils Omagh on behalf of his O'Neill allies.

1510
Kildare confirmed as lord deputy.

1513
Death of Great Earl of Kildare from gunshot

1534

wounds. Succeeded as ninth earl by his son Gearóid Óg (Young Gerald), who is also appointed lord deputy.

1519
Kildare summoned to English court.

1520
Thomas Howard, earl of Surrey, accompanied by 500 troops, arrives as lord lieutenant.

1523
Kildare returns to Ireland.

1524
Kildare reappointed deputy.

1530
William Skeffington appointed lord deputy.

1531
Henry VIII head of the Church of England.

1532
Kildare deputy once more.

1534
Henry VIII excommunicated by pope. Kildare once more summoned to English court, leaves his son "Silken" Thomas, Lord Offaly, in his place. He is arrested and held in the Tower of London, where he dies later in the year.

1534
Silken Thomas denounces Henry VIII's religious reforms and withdraws his allegiance to the crown. His followers murder Archbishop Alen of Dublin.

1534
Skeffington reappointed lord deputy. Silken Thomas summoned to London. He declines to go, succeeds his dead father as tenth earl of Kildare and concludes a truce with Skeffington.

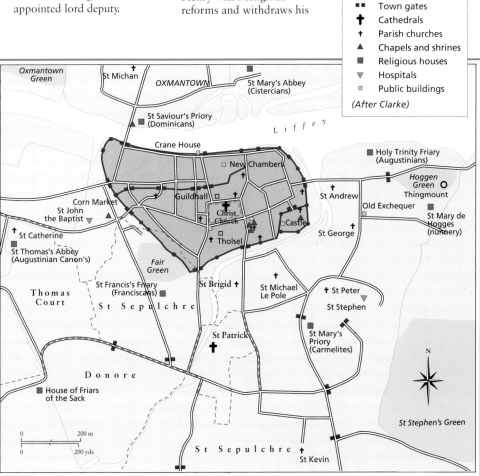

Dublin, 1170–1542

- - - Liberties borders
━●━ Town wall with towers
■■ Town gates
✝ Cathedrals
† Parish churches
▲ Chapels and shrines
■ Religious houses
▽ Hospitals
▫ Public buildings

(After Clarke)

Oxmantown Green
St Michan
OXMANTOWN
St Mary's Abbey (Cistercians)
St Saviour's Priory (Dominicans)
L i f f e y
Crane House
Holy Trinity Friary (Augustinians)
New Chambers
Hoggen Green
Thingmount
Guildhall
St Andrew
Old Exchequer
Corn Market
St John the Baptist
Christ Church
Castle
St George
St Mary de Hogges (nunnery)
St Catherine
Tholsel
St Thomas's Abbey (Augustinian Canon's)
Fair Green
St Francis's Friary (Franciscans)
St Brigid
St Michael Le Pole
St Peter
St Stephen
Thomas Court
St Sepulchre
St Patrick
St Mary's Priory (Carmelites)
N
Donore
House of Friars of the Sack
St Stephen's Green
0   200 m
0   200 yds
St Sepulchre
St Kevin

EARLY MODERN IRELAND – Tudor Conquest

Henry VIII of England during whose reign (1509-47) the Reformation began in Ireland and under whom Ireland was raised to the status of kingdom in 1541.

THE LORDSHIP of Ireland remained a formal fact of life until 1541. The Norman families who had established themselves in Ireland following 1169 came to dominate the south and east of the island. The rich limestone plains and river valleys were their strongholds: they introduced feudalism, primogeniture and patronised reforming church orders like the Cistercians. They had no presence in Ulster west of the Bann and their numbers in Connacht were low.

In time, inter-marriage and cultural mixing between Norman and Gael produced a hybrid society in which differences between the two ethnic groups were diluted without ever completely disappearing.

In the late middle ages, the three great Norman families were the two branches of the FitzGeralds – the earls of Kildare and Desmond – and the Butlers, earls of Ormond. Between them, they controlled most of Ireland south of a line from Dublin to Galway. The Kildare FitzGeralds, from the 1470s the hereditary lords deputy for the crown in Ireland, maintained marriage and patronage networks right up to the borders of Ulster.

Given the problems of distance and communication, this policy of devolution made sense. Only two kings – John in 1210 and Richard II twice in the 1390s – ever visited Ireland. It was easier to govern through lords deputy. But what seemed like sensible devolution to London looked more like a medieval form of home rule or autonomy in Ireland. In effect, the earls of Kildare had palatinate powers. Although they always ruled in the king's name, the relationship was reciprocally convenient. Medieval kings needed regional deputies in peripheral lands: the era of unitary national kingdoms lay in the future.

It was the development of such kingdoms that broke the mould in early modern Ireland. First England, then France and later Spain developed a more consolidated and centralised form of government, focused on the authority and person of the monarch and characterised by increasing uniformity of taxation, the suppression of palatine jurisdictions at the territorial margins and the assertion of royal power by armed force. The whole process took a century and more to reach fulfilment, but in England it started with Henry VIII.

Henry reigned from 1509 to 1547. He was a child of the Renaissance, that revolutionary tumult in European sensibility that introduced classical architecture, perspective painting, printing, the revival of classical learning, individual portraiture, the European voyages of discovery, the heliocentric understanding of the universe, the development of modern cartography and a general sense that the world was being made anew, or at least thought anew.

The Renaissance ideal of kingship was vastly more assertive than the medieval ideal had been. It asserted the dynamic personality of the monarch as the agent for a more aggressively centralised state. Henry VIII's embrace of this model was most evident in his break with Rome. His desire to divorce his wife, Catherine of Aragon, in favour of Anne Boleyn, was denied by the pope. Henry responded by establishing himself as the head of an independent English church, dissolving monastic establishments and diverting their revenues to the state. He crushed provincial resistance to his new order and laid the basis for England's embrace of Protestantism.

The Protestant Reformation, dating from 1517, was the greatest schism in the history of Latin Christianity. It coincided with Henry's break with Rome and his increasing policy of centralisation. In Ireland, that policy put pressure on the earls of Kildare. The ninth earl was summoned to London in 1534, while his son "Silken Thomas" FitzGerald, Lord Offaly, staged a protest in Dublin against royal policy that developed into outright rebellion. It was almost certainly intended to remind London of the traditional refrain that Ireland could not be governed without Kildare power. Instead of the conventional response – negotiation and compromise – Henry faced down the Kildares, executed Silken Thomas (his father had already died in the Tower of London in dubious circumstances) and declared the vast Kildare estates forfeit to the crown.

It was the end of medieval Ireland. Direct rule by English governors replaced devolved rule by Hiberno-Norman grandees. In 1541 the kingdom of Ireland was proclaimed, removing any ambiguity as to the nature of the English claim to the island. The policy of surrender and regrant substituted English land titles for Gaelic ones. The confused mixture of religious reformation, state centralisation, land law reform and advancing anglicisation was the basic dynamic of Irish history from 1534 until the mid seventeenth century. Aggressive New English (Protestant) adventurers, evangelists and administrators were resisted by the Gaelic chiefs and the Hiberno-Normans – or, as they are now best styled, the Old English. Both the Gaels and the Old English remained Catholic. From the very first, therefore, Irish Protestantism was associated with the newly aggressive and centralising Tudor state, while Catholicism was a shield for traditional autonomies.

Until the early seventeenth century Gaelic society in many regions of Ireland remained relatively unaffected by the policy of anglicisation. Eventually, however, the power of the Gaelic chieftains and their cultural and social practices succumbed to the influence of newly-settled officials and planters.

1535

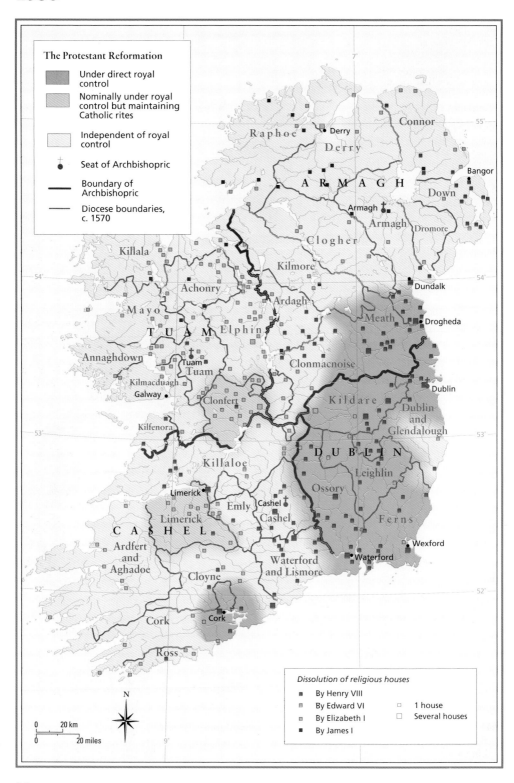

The Protestant Reformation

Under direct royal control

Nominally under royal control but maintaining Catholic rites

Independent of royal control

Seat of Archbishopric

Boundary of Archbishopric

Diocese boundaries, c. 1570

Raphoe Derry Connor
Derry
ARMAGH Bangor
Down
Armagh
Armagh Dromore
Clogher
Killala
Kilmore Dundalk
Achonry
Ardagh Meath Drogheda
Mayo
TUAM Elphin
Annaghdown Clonmacnoise
Tuam
Tuam
Kilmacduagh Kildare Dublin
Galway Dublin and Glendalough
Clonfert
Kilfenora
DUBLIN
Killaloe Leighlin
Limerick Ossory Ferns
Emly Cashel
Limerick Cashel
CASHEL Wexford
Ardfert and Aghadoe Waterford
Waterford and Lismore
Cloyne
Cork Cork
Ross

N

0   20 km
0   20 miles

Dissolution of religious houses

By Henry VIII
By Edward VI   ☐ 1 house
By Elizabeth I   ☐ Several houses
By James I

1565

1535

Skeffington captures Maynooth Castle, a FitzGerald stronghold, in one of the first instances of a successful artillery assault in Irish history.

1535

Lord Leonard Gray arrives in Ireland at the head of a royal army.

1536

First meeting of Irish "Reformation parliament" passes Act of Supremacy and attaints the Kildare FitzGeralds. The Act of Supremacy formally establishes the Church of Ireland as the state church independent of Rome, with the monarch at its head.

1537

Silken Thomas and five of his uncles executed at Tyburn, London.

1538

Augustinian house of All Hallowes in Dublin the first Irish religious establishment to be suppressed, i.e., surrendered to the crown. It later provides the site for Trinity College.

1539

Dissolution of religious houses advances apace.

1540

Sir Anthony St Leger lord deputy.

1541

Beginning of policy of "surrender and regrant", whereby titles held under Irish law are surrendered to the crown and re-granted under English law.

1541

Formal declaration of the kingdom of Ireland, ending

the lordship that had existed since 1177. The king of England henceforth to be the king of Ireland.

1542

First Jesuit missionaries in Ireland.

1542

Conn Bacach O'Neill, heir to the historic partimony of Uí Néill, surrenders and is appointed first earl of Tyrone.

1543

O'Briens appointed earls of Thomond, Burkes earls of Clanrickard under policy of surrender and regrant.

1547

Death of Henry VIII; succeeded by Edward VI, a minor.

1549

Order made for the use of the Book of Common Prayer in Ireland.

1551

An edition of the Book of Common Prayer becomes the first book to be printed in Ireland.

1553

Death of Edward VI, succeeded by his half-sister Mary, a Catholic.

1554

Restoration of earldom of Kildare to Gerald FitzGerald, half-brother of Silken Thomas, who succeeds as eleventh earl.

1556

Plans issued for the plantation of Leix and Offaly (Queen's and King's Counties).

1558

Death of Queen Mary; succeeded by her half-sister Elizabeth, a Protestant.

1558

Murder of Matthew, illegitimate son of Conn Bacach O'Neill and baron of Dungannon, heir to the earldom of Tyrone on instructions of Shane O'Neill, Conn's eldest legimate son, who had claimed the Gaelic title of O'Neill but also wished to inherit the earldom of Tyrone as was his entitlement in proper form.

1560

Irish Act of Supremacy reasserts the position of the Church of Ireland as the state church.

1560

David Wolfe SJ, born in Limerick, appointed papal nuncio to Ireland.

1560

Earl of Sussex, lord deputy, ordered to make war on Shane O'Neill.

1561

O'Neill proclaimed a traitor; Sussex campaigns in Ulster.

1562

Shane O'Neill submits to queen in London in February, but has rebelled again by November. Brian O'Neill, second baron Dungannon, murdered on Shane's orders.

1563

Battle of Tullaghogue: Sussex defeats Shane O'Neill, who submits again.

1565

Battle of Affane, Co. Waterford, in which the encroaching forces of the earl of Desmond are defeated by those of the earl of Ormond, "Black Tom" Butler: the last such

1565

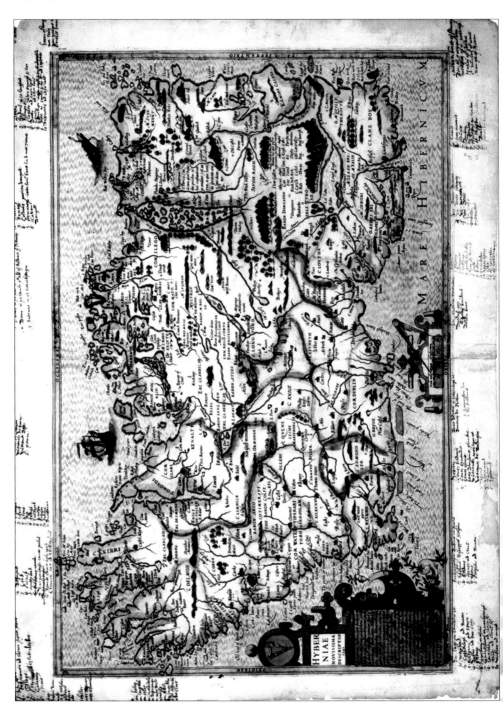

Ireland engraved by Van den Keere, in England in 1591, published by Hondius. More accurate than the well known Ortelius map published a year later. This is reproduced from one of only two surviving copies.

battle between great private magnates in Irish history.

1565
Shane O'Neill defeats the MacDonnells of Antrim at the battle of Glenshesk.

1565
The MacCarthy Mór created earl of Clancarthy.

1566
Shane O'Neill seeks alliances in Scotland and France, is declared a traitor and burns Armagh cathedral.

1567
Shane O'Neill defeated in battle by O'Donnells of Tír Chonaill (Donegal) and murdered by MacDonnells of Antrim. Turlough Luineach O'Neill succeeds to the Gaelic chieftaincy.

1568
Hugh O'Neill, brother of the murdered Brian, inaugurated as baron Dungannon.

1569
Beginnings of the Desmond rebellions: James Fitzmaurice FitzGerald, brother of the earl, together with dissident Butlers, conduct series of campaigns against New English incursions in the south.

1569
Return of "Black Tom" Butler, tenth earl of Ormond, from a visit to England. A Protestant and a favourite of the Queen – a distant cousin – he detaches the dissident Butlers from the Fitzmaurice rebellion.

1570
Sir John Perrot appointed president of Munster, to

drive forward a more vigorous policy of New English incursion and to defeat Fitzmaurice.

1571
Fitzmaurice sacks Kilmallock.

1571
Aibidil Gaoidheilge & Caiticiosma/Gaelic Alphabet & Catechism first book to be printed in Irish in Ireland.

1573
James Fitzmaurice FitzGerald submits to Sir John Perrot. Earl of Desmond arrested and imprisoned, but escapes.

1574
Desmond submits to lord deputy Fitzwilliam.

1575
James Fitzmaurice FitzGerald sails for Europe to seek alliances in support of Catholic rebellion in Munster.

1579
James Fitzmaurice FitzGerald, together with the papal legate, Nicholas Sanders, lands on the northern side of the Dingle peninsula, at Smerwick harbour, and establish Dún an Óir/The Golden Fort. They bear papal letters absolving the Irish lords from allegiance to Queen Elizabeth and call for a war to restore Catholicism as the state religion in Ireland.

1579
Fitzmaurice killed in skirmish in Co. Limerick.

1579
The earl of Desmond joins the rebellion.

1580
Lord Grey de Wilton

arrives as lord deputy. He is defeated in the Wicklow hills by Fiach MacHugh O'Byrne.

1580
Papal reinforcements arrive at Smerwick. Grey de Wilton and earl of Ormond move against them and massacre the garrison.

1581
Publication of John Derricke's *The Image of Irelande*, an important if partial account of contemporary Ireland and in particular of Gaelic mores and manners.

1582
Famine in Munster as a result of Grey de Wilton's scorched earth policy.

1583
Desmond rebellion ends with the murder of the earl of Desmond near Tralee, Co. Kerry. This marked the end of the earldom; its lands were declared forfeit to the crown and were settled by New English adventurers as part of the plantation of Munster.

1584
Sir Richard Bingham president of Connacht, vigorous promoter of New English interests.

1585
Composition of Connacht replaces English customs and laws for Irish.

1587
Sir Walter Raleigh granted 40,000 acres in east Munster.

1587
Hugh O'Neill, brother of the murdered Brian, earl of Tyrone.

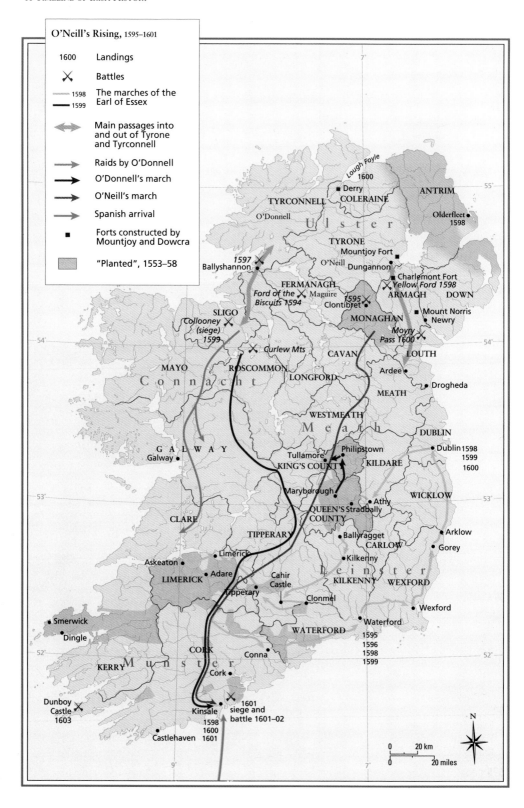

O'Neill's Rising, 1595–1601

1600	Landings
✕	Battles
—— 1598	The marches of the
—— 1599	Earl of Essex
⟷	Main passages into and out of Tyrone and Tyrconnell
→	Raids by O'Donnell
→	O'Donnell's march
→	O'Neill's march
→	Spanish arrival
■	Forts constructed by Mountjoy and Dowcra
▨	"Planted", 1553–58

Lough Foyle 1600
Derry
ANTRIM
TYRCONNELL
COLERAINE
O'Donnell
Ulster
Olderfleet 1598
TYRONE
Mountjoy Fort
O'Neill Dungannon
1597
Ballyshannon
Charlemont Fort
Yellow Ford 1598
FERMANAGH
Ford of the Biscuits 1594
Maguire
1595 Clontibret
ARMAGH DOWN
SLIGO
Collooney (siege) 1599
MONAGHAN
Mount Norris Newry
Moyry Pass 1600
Curlew Mts
CAVAN
LOUTH
MAYO
ROSCOMMON
Connacht
LONGFORD
Ardee
Drogheda
MEATH
WESTMEATH
Meath
GALWAY
Galway
Tullamore Philipstown
KING'S COUNTY
KILDARE
DUBLIN
Dublin 1598 1599 1600
Maryborough
Athy
WICKLOW
CLARE
QUEEN'S COUNTY
Stradbally
TIPPERARY
Ballyragget
CARLOW
Arklow
Gorey
Limerick
Kilkenny
Leinster
Askeaton
Adare
LIMERICK
Cahir Castle
KILKENNY WEXFORD
Tipperary
Clonmel
Wexford
Smerwick
Dingle
CORK
Conna
WATERFORD
Waterford 1595 1596 1598 1599
KERRY
Munster
Cork
Dunboy Castle 1603
Kinsale 1598 1600 1601
1601 siege and battle 1601–02
Castlehaven

0   20 km
0   20 miles

N

1599

1588

Spanish armada ships wrecked on western coast.

1591

Hugh O'Neill, earl of Tyrone, elopes with Mabel Bagenal, sister of Sir Henry Bagenal, the New English army commander in Ulster.

1591

Red Hugh O'Donnell, Gaelic lord of Tír Chonaill, escapes from Dublin Castle where he had been held prisoner since 1587.

1592

Foundation of Trinity College, Dublin.

1593

Turlough Luineach O'Neill resigns the chieftaincy of the O'Neills in favour of Hugh O'Neill, earl of Tyrone, who now joins both the Gaelic and English titles in his person.

1593

Government pressure on Gaelic kingdoms in southern Ulster results in formation of a Catholic coalition led by the archbishop of Armagh, Edmund Magauran, who is killed in battle by Sir Richard Bingham.

1594

Government forces, aided by Gaelic dissidents, capture the Maguire stronghold of Enniskillen, a vital strategic position on the approaches of south-west Ulster.

1595

Red Hugh O'Donnell and Hugh Maguire recapture Enniskillen.

1595

Hugh O'Neill, earl of Tyrone, destroys the fort and bridge on the Blackwater near Armagh.

1595

Tyrone defeats Sir Henry Bagenal at the battle of Clontibret. He is declared a traitor to the crown.

1596

King Philip II of Spain offers help to earl of Tyrone, who attempts to forge alliance with Gaelic chiefs in Munster. Spanish ships with arms and munitions land at Killybegs, Co. Donegal.

1597

Death of Wicklow chieftain Fiach MacHugh O'Byrne, long a thorn in the government's side.

1597

Red Hugh O'Donnell defeats government troops at Ballyshannon.

1598

Battle of the Yellow Ford, the greatest Irish success of the Nine Years' War. A force under Tyrone and Hugh Maguire routs government troops under Sir Hugh Bagenal, who is killed.

1599

Earl of Essex lord lieutenant.

1599

Essex defeated in battle at the Pass of the Plumes by Irish force under Owney O'More of Leix, but proceeds to accept submissions of Lords Mountgarret and Cahir.

1599

Phelim MacFeagh O'Byrne

Hugh O'Neill, earl of Tyrone. He was the leading political and military figure on the Gaelic Irish side during the Nine Years' War.

1599

inflicts heavy defeat on English force under Sir Henry Harrington at Deputy's Pass, Co. Wicklow.

1599

Tyrone receives more military supplies from Spain.

1599

Battle of the Curlew Mountains in Connacht: Brian Óg O'Rourke defeats Sir Conyers Clifford, president of Connacht, who is killed.

1599

Tyrone issues appeal to "the Catholics of the towns of Ireland to come and join with me against the enemies of God and of our poor country". This appeal, directed at the Old English (i.e. Catholics of Hiberno-Norman origin) to join in a Catholic crusade beside the Gaelic forces already in the field, gets little response.

1600

Charles Blount, Lord Mountjoy, lord deputy. Sir George Carew president of Munster.

1600

Mountjoy threatens southern Ulster. Sir Henry Dowcra sails from Carrickfergus to Lough Foyle and establishes Culmore fort on the site of the later city of Derry.

The Royal Army meet the combined armies of Tyrone and O'Donnell together with their Spanish allies at Kinsale on Christmas eve in 1601.

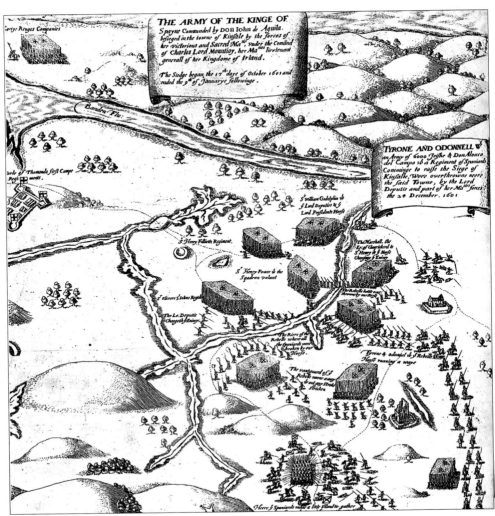

1608

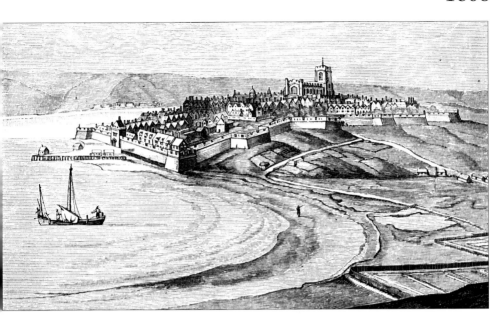

1600

Mountjoy campaigns in midlands of Leinster, kills Owney O'More.

1600

Battle of Moyry Pass: Mountjoy forces his way through into south-east Ulster despite strong resistance from Tyrone.

1600

More Spanish aid landed in Co. Donegal.

1600

Niall Garbh O'Donnell, a cousin of Red Hugh, joined Sir Henry Dowcra.

1601

Spanish fleet under the command of Don Juan del Aguila arrives at Kinsale, Co. Cork.

1601

Mountjoy invests Kinsale.

1601

Tyrone and Red Hugh O'Donnell, having marched separately from Ulster, join forces and attack Mountjoy.

Battle of Kinsale: Mountjoy routs the joint forces of the Ulster chiefs, effectively ending the Nine Years' War.

1602

Mountjoy invades Ulster, destroys the ancestral inaugural chair of the O'Neills at Tullaghoge.

1603

Death of Queen Elizabeth; succeeded by James I, the first of the Stuarts. Tyrone surrenders to Mountjoy at Mellifont.

1604

Charter for the incorporation of the town of Derry.

1605

Sir Arthur Chichester lord deputy.

1605

Proclamation against toleration in religion, ordering all laity to attend divine service in the established church; fines levied on defaulters, mainly Old English landowners

The modern town of Derry was founded under a royal charter granted to a number of companies in the City of London in 1613 (thus the more formal name of Londonderry). A key moment in the Plantation of Ulster, the foundation of the walled town replaced an earlier Gaelic settlement that had had its origins in a Columban monastic site.

and townsmen; order for priests – specifically Jesuits – to leave Ireland.

1606

Sir John Davies attorney-general.

1607

Flight of the Earls. Hugh O'Neill, earl of Tyrone, and others of the Ulster Gaelic aristocracy leave for the continent.

1608

Plans laid for the plantation of escheated lands in Ulster.

43

1610

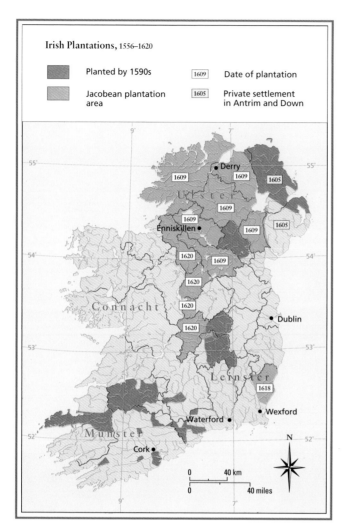

Irish Plantations, 1556–1620

Planted by 1590s

Jacobean plantation area

| 1609 | Date of plantation

| 1605 | Private settlement in Antrim and Down

1610
Agreement between the English privy council and the city of London for the plantation of the area around Derry.

1612
Charter incorporating Dungannon, the first plantation town in Ulster thus created.

1613
Charters incorporating the cities of Belfast and Derry and the town of Coleraine.

1616
Death of Hugh O'Neill, earl of Tyrone, in Rome.

1620
Richard Boyle created first earl of Cork.

1621
Plantation schemes extended to midlands.

1622
Death of Miler McGrath, Church of Ireland

archbishop of Cashel, one of the longest-lived and most assiduous pluralists, opportunists and denominational trimmers of the age. He had originally been a Franciscan friar and Catholic bishop of Down & Connor.

1625
Death of King James I, succeeded by his son Charles I.

1628
Charles I offers a series of concessions – principally aimed at the Old English – in return for subsidies of £120,000 to finance the wars with France and Spain. Known as The Graces, they were subsequently dishonoured by the king.

1629
Dublin authorities raid Franciscan chapel and suppress sixteen other Catholic religious houses in the city, prompting widespread rioting in protest.

1631
Algerine pirates from the Barbary Coast in North Africa sack the town of Baltimore, Co. Cork.

1632
Appointment of Wentworth as lord deputy.

1634
Seathrún Céitinn/Geoffrey Keating completes his *Foras Feasa ar Éireann*/Groundwork of Knowledge of Ireland, a narrative history of Ireland from earliest times to the arrival of the Normans.

1634

Under pressure from Wentworth, convocation of the Church of Ireland accepts the 39 Articles of the Church of England.

1636

Completion of *Annála Ríoghachta Éireann*/Annals of the Kingdom of Ireland, better known as the *Annals of the Four Masters*.

1637

First exploitation of coal mines at Castlecomer, Co. Kilkenny.

1638

Adoption of the Scots national covenant against the religious innovations of Charles I begins the long process of destabilisation that leads to revolution.

1639

Wentworth summoned back to London to help deal with growing national crisis.

1640

Wentworth raises an Irish army to assist Charles I against Scots Presbyterian rebels.

1641

Wentworth, having been attainted by the English parliament, is executed. Parliament now in open revolt against the crown.

1641

James Butler, twelfth earl of Ormond, takes control of royal forces in Ireland.

1641

Insurrection in Ulster. Although not intended as a sectarian crusade, it soon degenerated into one, as officers lost control of their men. In effect, it became a jacquerie against the Plantation of Ulster.

Thousands of settlers are massacred, many in circumstances of great cruelty.

1641

Ulster rebels move south, capturing Dundalk, Newry and other towns in south Ulster. The rebellion spreads south to the midlands: troops under Rory O'More of Leix defeat government forces at Julianstown, Co. Meath.

James I in 1621 from a portrait by David Mytens. King of England from 1603 and Scotland (as James VI) from 1567. The son of Mary Queen of Scots and Lord Darnley, he succeeded on his mother's abdication from the Scottish throne, assumed power in 1583, established a strong centralised authority, and in 1589 married Anne of Denmark.

1641

1641

Historic alliance formed between Old English lords of the Pale and the Ulster rebels in defence of their common religion, the first such confessional union across ethnic lines in Irish history. The proximate cause is the growing pressure from radical Protestantism represented

Munro arrive in Ulster to aid their beleaguered Presbyterian co-religionists.

1642

First regularly formed presbytery in Ireland meets at Carrickfergus.

1642

Owen Roe O'Neill, a nephew of Hugh O'Neill and a general in the service of the Spanish crown in

of Irish Catholics, known thereafter as the Confederation of Kilkenny.

1643

Truce agreed between Ormond on behalf of the king and the Confederation of Kilkenny.

1643

Ormond appointed lord lieutenant.

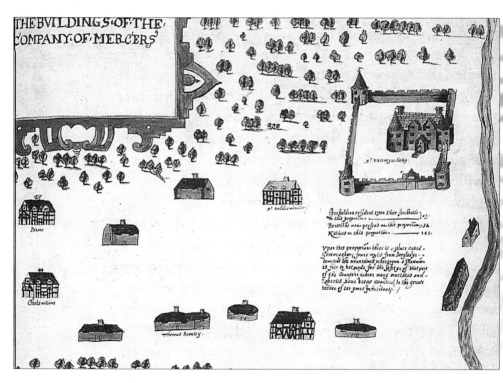

A contemporary plan of Mercers' settlement in Derry made during the plantation of Ulster.

by the English parliament and the New English element in the Irish government.

1642

Ormond defeats rebel forces at Kilrush, Co. Clare.

1642

Scots troops under Robert

Flanders, returns to Ireland.

1642

Beginning of English civil war.

1642

A meeting of lay and clerical leaders at Kilkenny establishes a confederation

1644

Munro's Scots army takes Belfast.

1644

Murrough O'Brien, Lord Inchiquin, abandons Ormond's royalists, declares for parliament and is appointed parliamentary Lord President of Munster.

1645

Sir Charles Coote follows

1647

0   20 km

0   20 miles

NE Liberties
of Coleraine

INISHOWEN

NW Liberties
of Derry

COLERAINE

DOE   FANAD

TIRKEERAN

PORTLOUGH   DERRY

KEENAGHT   ANTRIM

DONEGAL   LOUGHINSHOLIN

LIFFORD

STRABANE

BOYLAGH

TYRONE   MOUNTJOY   Lough
Neagh

TIRHUGH   OMAGH

LURG   Lough
Erne   DUNGANNON

CLOGHER   ONEILLAND

MAGHERABOY   COOLE AND
TIRKENNEDY

FERMANAGH   ARMAGH   DOWN

CLANAWLEY   MAGHERA-
STEPHANA   TIRANNY   ARMAGH

CLANKELLY   FEWS

TULLYHAW   KNOCKNINNY

SLIGO   MONAGHAN   ORIOR

TULLYGARVEY

LOUGHTEE

LEITRIM   CAVAN   CLANKEE   LOUTH

MAYO   TULLYHUNCO

CLANMAHON

ROSCOMMON   CASTLERAHAN

LONGFORD

N

Ulster Plantations, 1609

///// Subject to earlier settlement	English undertakers (estates of 2,000, 1,500 and 1,000 acres, with English or Scottish tenants exclusively)
Scottish undertakers (estates of 2,000, 1,500 and 1,000 acres, with English or Scottish tenants exclusively)	Servitors and Natives (Irish tenants permitted in certain cases)
Exceptional area	
Unplanted area	

(after Moody and Hunter)

suit and is appointed Lord
President of Connacht.

1645

Giovanni Batista Rinuccini,
archbishop of Fermo,
arrives in Ireland as papal
nuncio.

1646

First "Ormond Peace",
negotiated by the lord
lieutenant. Its aim was to
join Irish Protestant
royalists and the
Confederate Catholics in
united support for the king
and against parliament. In
return for their support,
the Confederates were
promised the Graces and
the repeal of Poynings Law.

1646

Under pressure from
Rinuccini, the

Confederation of Kilkenny
rejects the Ormond Peace.

1646

Owen Roe O'Neill routs
the Scots under Munro at
the battle of Benburb, the
greatest Confederate
military success of the war.

1647

Parliamentary army under
Colonel Michael Jones

1647

Sir Phelim O'Neill. On the evening of 22 October 1641, Sir Phelim and his co-conspirators seized Charlemont Castle claiming not to be in rebellion against the king but protecting him against "evil councillors" and producing a forged royal commission to vindicate their action.

lands near Dublin. Its first engagement brings a victory at Dungan's Hill against Confederate forces under Thomas Preston.

1647
Ormond agrees to surrender Dublin to the parliamentarians and withdraws to England.

1647
In Munster, Inchiquin's parliamentary forces sack Cashel and rout the Munster Confederates under Lord Taaffe at Knocknanuss near Kanturk in north Co. Cork.

1648
Inchiquin rejoins royalists. He begins negotiations for a truce with the Supreme Council of the Conferation.

1648
Confederation splits between those, encouraged by Rinuccini and Owen Roe O'Neill, who oppose the Inchiquin peace – wishing to push Catholic claims more strongly – and those who support it.

1648
Ormond returns.

1649
Ormond concludes a second peace with the Confederates.

1649
Execution of King Charles I.

1649
Rinuccini flees Ireland.

1649
Oliver Cromwell appointed commander of the parliamentary army in Ireland.

1649
Royalists capture Drogheda.

1649
Jones' parliamentary army defeats Ormond at Rathmines, clearing the way for Cromwell's arrival. He lands in August.

1649
Cromwell takes Drogheda and slaughters the garrison and civilians.

1649
Cromwell takes Wexford; another massacre.

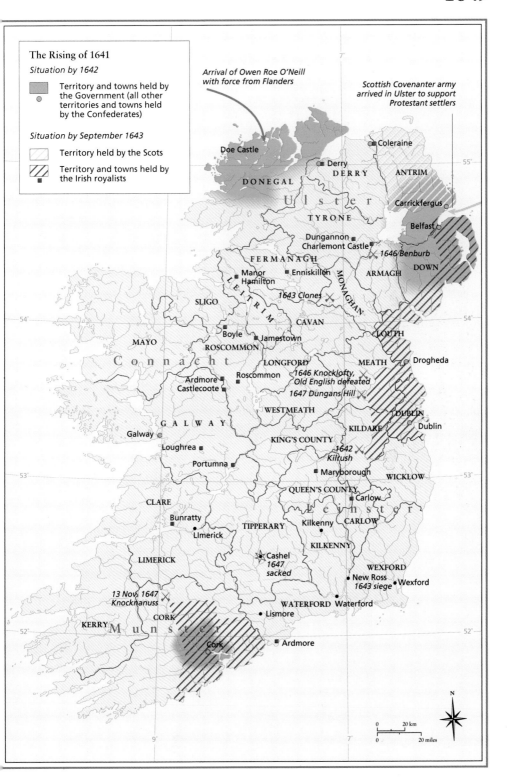

The Rising of 1641

Situation by 1642

Territory and towns held by the Government (all other territories and towns held by the Confederates)

Situation by September 1643

Territory held by the Scots

Territory and towns held by the Irish royalists

Arrival of Owen Roe O'Neill with force from Flanders

Scottish Covenanter army arrived in Ulster to support Protestant settlers

Doe Castle

Coleraine

Derry

DERRY

ANTRIM

DONEGAL

Ulster

TYRONE

Carrickfergus

Belfast

Dungannon
Charlemont Castle

1646 Benburb

FERMANAGH

DOWN

Manor
Hamilton

Enniskillen

ARMAGH

MONAGHAN

SLIGO

LEITRIM

1643 Clones

CAVAN

LOUTH

Boyle

Jamestown

MAYO

ROSCOMMON

LONGFORD

MEATH

Drogheda

Connacht

Roscommon

1646 Knocklofty,
Old English defeated

Ardmore
Castlecoote

1647 Dungans Hill

WESTMEATH

GALWAY

Galway

KILDARE

Dublin

DUBLIN

Loughrea

KING'S COUNTY

1642
Kilrush

Portumna

Maryborough

WICKLOW

CLARE

QUEEN'S COUNTY

Carlow

Leinster

Bunratty

Kilkenny

CARLOW

Limerick

TIPPERARY

KILKENNY

LIMERICK

Cashel
1647
sacked

WEXFORD

New Ross
1643 siege

Wexford

13 Nov 1647
Knocknanuss

KERRY

Munster

CORK

WATERFORD

Waterford

Lismore

Cork

Ardmore

N

0   20 km
0   20 miles

Cromwell

Oliver Cromwell, commander of the Puritan New Model Army, religious zealot, one of England's national heroes and the most reviled name in Irish history.

THE TUDOR re-conquest of Ireland was incomplete. The key question in early modern Europe was that of religious allegiance. Under Elizabeth I (r.1558–1603), the daughter of Henry VIII, Protestantism triumphed in England, Scotland and Wales but Ireland remained stubbornly Catholic. Despite the incursions of New English landowners like Richard Boyle, first earl of Cork, most land remained in Catholic hands at the end of the sixteenth century. The defeat of Catholic rebellions in Munster in the 1580s and in Ulster – the Nine Years' War of 1594–1603 – opened the way for new Protestant settlement, without altering the overall picture.

However, the establishment of a concerted and successful Protestant plantation in Ulster following the final defeat and flight of the Gaelic lords in 1607 was significant. It established a coherent Protestant redoubt in the northern province, in contrast to scattered Protestant settlement in the three southern provinces. Once again, but in an ironically inverted way, Ulster was to be the odd-man-out in the Irish provincial line-up: in 1590, the most Gaelic province, in 1610 the least so.

The question of confessional allegiance was important because of a basic assumption made in all early modern states: in order to avoid potentially lethal religious wars, states sought religious conformity. The newly united kingdom of Spain expelled Muslims and Jews; France was torn by civil wars of religion between Catholics and Huguenots; as early as 1555, the religious peace of Augsburg attempted to stabilise the precarious Catholic–Protestant balance in the Holy Roman Empire with the formula that in any given kingdom the religion of the ruler would automatically become that of his subjects.

In England, the presence of a sister-kingdom to the west in which the Catholic interest remained dominant was a reproach and a security threat. England's traditional enemy, France, was a Catholic kingdom. The leading European power of the time, Spain, was even more so, and took England so seriously that it attempted an invasion in 1588. The fact that Ireland was a potential Catholic beachhead for future continental invasion forces was never far from English minds.

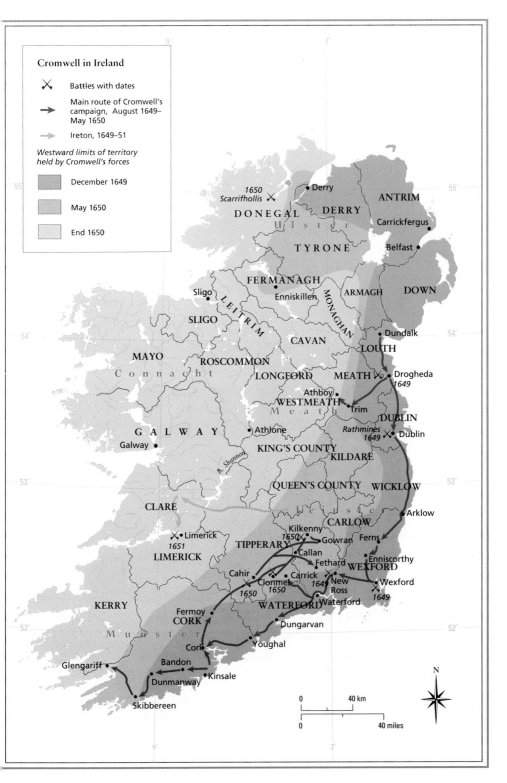

Cromwell in Ireland

✗ Battles with dates

➡ Main route of Cromwell's campaign, August 1649– May 1650

➡ Ireton, 1649–51

Westward limits of territory held by Cromwell's forces

December 1649

May 1650

End 1650

When James I, the first of the Stuarts, succeeded in 1603, Catholics still owned the vast majority of all Irish land. Even after the Plantation of Ulster, they still controlled most of the land in the other three provinces. In an age when land meant power, Catholic landowners – now mainly Old English – remained a potent interest group. The Dublin administration was in the hands of the New English: relations between these Protestant parvenus and the settled Old English Catholics were increasingly tense.

Ireland in the first half of the seventeenth century involved a series of precarious relationships: between Protestant planters and Catholic tenants in Ulster; between Old and New English, and by extension between the crown and the Old English; within the Catholic community, between the Gaelic element and their spiritual champions, the Franciscans, and the Old English of the towns with their preference for the Counter-Reformation orthodoxies of the Jesuits.

The sensitive balance was upset by the Ulster rebellion of 1641, in which the dispossessed Catholics rose up against the planters. Although later accounts exaggerated the scale of the killings for propaganda purposes, there is no doubt that many atrocities were committed. The whole Irish situation then became caught up in the confusing events of the English Civil War. When the dust finally settled in 1649, King Charles I had lost his head and Oliver Cromwell was master of England and Scotland.

The situation in Ireland was at least as confused as in England, with royalists, parliamentarians, Catholic Confederates and Ulster Presbyterians all in arms during the 1640s. Cromwell determined to put an end to this chaos and to avenge the atrocities of 1641 in Ulster. He landed in Dublin in August 1649. When he left, ten months later, he had used his peerless New Model Army to sweep aside all opposition. He massacred the garrisons at Drogheda and Wexford and by the time of his return to England, there was only a mopping-up operation left to complete. For the first time ever, Ireland was under firm and total English control.

Cromwell was a Protestant zealot. He determined to clear as many Catholic landowners as possible off their lands and to plant reliable English Protestants there instead. He ordered that all Catholic landowners in the rich provinces of Munster and Leinster must forfeit their lands and remove to Connacht, beyond the Shannon. The new Cromwellian planters were the antecedents of the eighteenth-century Protestant ascendancy. The dispossession of the Catholics was made without regard to their remote ethnic origins: Cromwell was the first person to disregard the ancient distinction between Gael and Old English, regarding Catholics as an undifferentiated mass, all of them complicit, more or less, in the Ulster horrors of 1641. The Cromwellian land confiscations set the pattern for Irish history for the next 250 years.

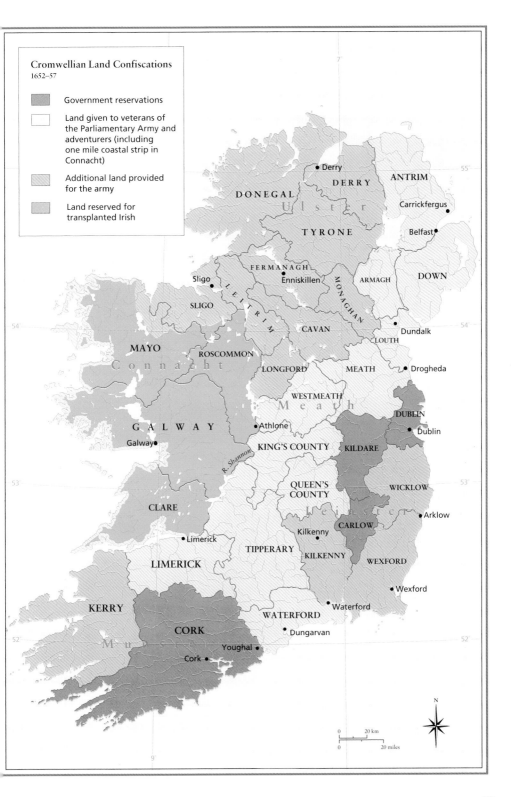

Cromwellian Land Confiscations
1652–57

- Government reservations
- Land given to veterans of the Parliamentary Army and adventurers (including one mile coastal strip in Connacht)
- Additional land provided for the army
- Land reserved for transplanted Irish

1650

The ruins of the manor house at Burntcourt (Clogheen), Co. Tipperary. Newly-built, it was burnt in 1650 lest it fall to the advancing Cromwellian army.

1650

Cromwell conquers Munster, returning to England leaving army in command of Henry Ireton.

1650

Ormond and other leading royalists, including Inchiquin, leave for France.

1651

Parliamentary commissioners take over government of Ireland.

1652

Last outposts of resistance surrender to Cromwellians, who now control all Ireland.

1653

Execution of Sir Phelim O'Neill, first military leader of the Ulster insurrection of 1641.

1653

Orders made for the conduct of civil and mapped surveys of Ireland, preparatory to land settlement.

1653

The English parliament identifies fourteen Irish counties, all east of the Shannon and the Bann, for plantation. Existing landowners were either executed or transported in the case of those to whom the greatest guilt was ascribed; others were merely dispossessed and removed west of the Shannon.

1654

William Petty appointed to conduct the mapped survey, known ever after as the Down Survey because it

was set down on maps rather than presented in tabular form.

1655

Governor of Dublin ordered to clear the city of Papists and to ship all priests not guilty of murder to Barbados.

1655

Henry Cromwell appointed major-general of the army in Ireland.

1656

Death of James Ussher, Church of Ireland archbishop of Armagh who had calculated the date of the Creation as 4004 BC. His extensive library – 10,000 volumes and priceless early manuscripts and codices – formed the basis of the library of Trinity College, Dublin.

1657

Legislation confirming the titles of the new Cromwellian planters.

1657

Legislation attainting all "rebels and papists" except for those who have removed beyond the Shannon. Suspected Catholics must renounce allegiance to the pope under oath and deny the doctrine of transubstantiation, failing which they forfeit two-thirds of any remaining lands.

1658

Death of Oliver Cromwell;

William Petty's Down Survey 1655–57. "The Parrish of Killmainham, County Dublin" by Robert Girdler.

succeeded by his feeble son Richard.

1659

On resignation of Richard Cromwell, three parliamentary commissioners appointed to govern Ireland.

1659

Henry Cromwell returns to England.

1659

Edmund O'Reilly, the Catholic archbishop of Armagh since 1657

(consecrated in Brussels) returns to Ireland.

1660

Restoration of Stuarts. Charles II proclaimed king of Ireland in Dublin, takes possession of his three kingdoms.

1660

An act granting a "general pardon, indemnity and oblivion" specifically excludes those who fomented the Ulster rising of 1641.

1660

King Charles II issues declaration confirming the security of land titles

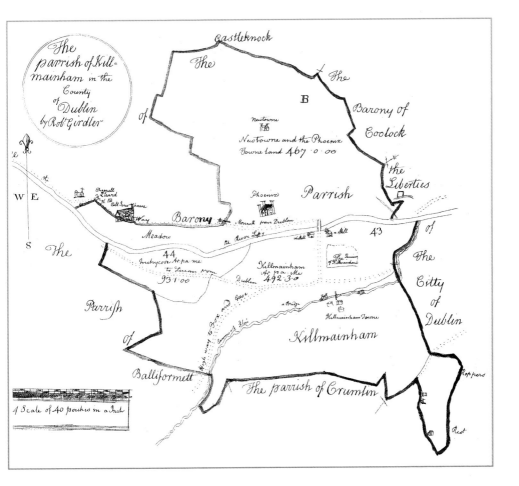

1661

James, Duke of Ormond, raised to the dukedom on the restoration of James II and made Lord Lieutenant of Ireland.

acquired under the Cromwellian land settlement, while wishing to make provision for "innocent papists".

1661

Re-establishment of the Church of Ireland.

1661

James Butler raised to a dukedom as first duke of Ormond and appointed lord lieutenant.

1661

First Irish parliament since 1641.

1662

Return of Ormond.

1662

Act of Settlement provided for the restoration of a small number of named "innocents" to their lands, but in general leaves the Cromwellian settlement intact.

1663

English Navigation Act forbids Irish exports to the colonies other than through English ports. A Cattle Act places limits on the importation of Irish cattle into England.

1665

Act of Explanation passed by Irish parliament to

resolve difficulties encountered in the workings of the Act of Settlement 1662. Cromwellian settlers, with some exception, surrendered one-third of their holdings to facilitate restoration of land to innocent Catholics.

1666

Act of Uniformity strengthens position of the established church.

1666

Mutiny of garrison at Carrickfergus suppressed by Lord Arran.

1667

Charter incorporating the Dublin College of Physicians.

1667

English legislation prohibits importation of Irish cattle and other livestock.

1669

Oliver Plunkett Catholic archbishop of Armagh; consecrated in Ghent.

1669

Ormond removed as lord lieutenant.

1670

Oliver Plunkett arrives in Ireland. He summons a synod of bishops which declares loyalty to the king.

1671

English Navigation Act prohibits the direct import of goods from the colonies into Ireland.

1672

First payment of regium donum, a royal grant in support of Presbyterian clergymen, is most notable evidence of short-lived experiment in religious toleration.

1673

Test Act requires all holders of public office to take communion in conformity to the usages of the established church; this effectively penalises observant Catholics and Dissenters.

1673

Proclamation banishing Catholic bishops and priests, and closing schools and religious houses.

1677

Return of Ormond as lord lieutenant.

1678

Titus Oates' "popish plot" unleashes a wave of hysteria in England. His allegations are accepted by the House of Lords. Further anti-Catholic measures proclaimed.

1678

Ormond closes all schools and religious houses and banishes clergy and bishops.

1679

Oliver Plunkett, Catholic archbishop of Armagh, arrested.

1680

Peter Talbot, Catholic archbishop of Dublin, dies in prison having been named by Titus Oates in his allegations.

1681

Oliver Plunkett executed in London following conviction for high treason on perjured evidence.

1684

Foundation of the Dublin Philosophical Society, forerunner of the Royal Dublin Society.

1684

Opening of Royal Hospital, Kilmainham; William Robinson, architect. The first great public building erected in the Irish capital since the Middle Ages.

1685

Death of Charles II; succeeded by his brother James II, last Catholic monarch of England to date.

1685

Richard Talbot, earl of Tyrconnell, succeeds Ormond as lord lieutenant.

1686

Earl of Clarendon lord lieutenant; Tyrconnell lieutenant-general of the army in Ireland.

1687

Tyrconnell lord deputy.

1687

Sir Alexander Fitton, a Roman Catholic, becomes lord chancellor of Ireland.

1688

Proposals to alter Cromwellian land settlement in favour of Catholics.

1688

Birth of a male heir to James II appears to secure the Catholic royal succession.

1688

Glorious Revolution in England: William III displaces James II, who flees to France.

1688

At Derry, city gates are closed against Catholic army under Lord Antrim.

1689

James II lands at Kinsale.

1689

Siege of Derry: for 105 days the beleaguered Protestant city holds out until the siege is broken by Williamite ships.

In 1684 the Royal Hospital at Kilmainham was opened, the first major new building in the expansion of Dublin.

1689

1701

1689

"Patriot parliament" in Dublin attended by James II, composed substantially of Old English Catholics. It enacted measures to undo the Cromwellian land settlement and restore the situation as at 1641. Christ Church cathedral, Dublin, restored to Catholic church.

1689

Marshal Schomberg arrives in Ulster at the head of Williamite army, besieges and captures Carrickfergus.

1690

William III arrives in Carrickfergus.

1690

Battle of the Boyne. The two kings and their armies meet in battle near Oldbridge, Co. Meath. The Williamites triumph. James flees. With over 60,000 troops deployed, it is the largest battle in Irish history. James returns to France.

1690

Siege of Limerick, which refuses to surrender to Williamites.

1690

Patrick Sarsfield, Jacobite commander, destroys the Williamite siege train at

Collins Barracks, Dublin, originally built in the early eighteenth century as the Royal Barracks. One of the first monumental buildings of the early Georgian period, the parade ground is the largest in Ireland. It was used by the Irish army until the 1990s, when it became part of the National Museum of Ireland.

Ballyneety, near Limerick, in a daring raid that results in the raising of the siege of Limerick.

1691

Athlone falls to the Williamites after siege.

1691

Battle of Aughrim, the decisive battle between Williamites and Jacobites, results in total victory for the former.

1691

Second siege of Limerick. Following a truce, the treaty of Limerick formally ends the war. The generous terms offered by the Williamite military commanders to the Jacobites enrage Irish Protestant opinion.

1691

Sarsfield and the "Wild Geese", generally officers of Old English background, leave to take service in the armies of Catholic powers on the continent.

1692

Williamite Irish House of Commons rejects a money bill prepared by the privy council and claims the sole right to initiate financial legislation.

1693

Death of Patrick Sarsfield, by now a French officer, at the battle of Landen.

1695

Act forbidding Catholics to educate their children abroad or to open schools in Ireland.

1697

Irish parliament finally approves the treaty of Limerick, but with material changes to the terms

A medal struck to commemorate the Protestant victories, 1690–91.

originally agreed. These changes and omissions were all to the disadvantage of Catholics.

1697

First of the major penal laws against Catholics enacted by the Irish parliament: "all papists exercising any ecclesiastical jurisdiction and all regulars of the popish clergy" to leave Ireland within the year.

1699

Woollen Act passed at Westminster bans export of Irish wool to any destination except England.

1701

Building of Royal Barracks, Dublin (later Collins Barracks) begins. Thomas Burgh, architect.

1701

Building of Marsh's Library, Dublin, the first public library in Dublin, named for Archbishop Narcissus Marsh, scholar and provost of TCD. Architect, Sir William Robinson.

1704

1704
"Act to Prevent the Further Growth of Popery", one of the key penal laws, enacted. It forbids Catholics to buy land; to lease it for longer than 31 years; obliges partible inheritance unless one son conforms to the Established Church, in which case he inherits all; provides a sacramental test for public office.

1711
Establishment of the Linen Board an important step in the development of this key industry, especially in Ulster.

1712
Building of Old Library, TCD, begins (completed 1732). Thomas Burgh, architect.

1713
Jonathan Swift dean of St Patrick's cathedral, Dublin.

1714
Treaty of Utrecht ends War of the Spanish Succession.

1714
Death of Queen Anne, last Stuart monarch, brings George I, the first of the Hanoverian line, to the thrones of England, Scotland and Ireland.

1715
William Conolly elected Speaker of the Irish House of Commons.

1718
Charitable Infirmary opens in Dublin (later Jervis St hospital), first such foundation in Britain or Ireland.

1719
Toleration Act removes some penal disabilities from Dissenters.

1720
Declaratory Act (also known as Sixth of George I) establishes the House of Lords in London as final court of appeal in all Irish litigation and asserts the legislative supremacy of London over Dublin.

1722
Wood's Halfpence. A patent to mint copper coins for Ireland was granted to the king's mistress, the duchess of Kendal, who sold it on to William Wood, an ironmonger. Fierce opposition in Ireland was based on a fear of worthless coinage fuelling inflation and eventually resulted in the withdrawal of the patent in 1725.

1724
Publication of Swift's *Drapier's Letters* in opposition to Wood's Halfpence.

1725
Dissident Presbyterians, who decline to conform to the Westminster Confession of Faith, form themselves into the Presbytery of Antrim.

1729
Foundation stone laid for new Parliament House in College Green, Dublin. Edward Lovett Pearce, architect.

1729
First publication of Swift's *Modest Proposal*, in which he satirically advocates the eating of Irish children as a measure of population control.

1731
Foundation of Dublin Society (Royal Dublin Society from 1820) "for improving husbandry, manufactures and other useful arts".

1736
First publication of *Dublin Daily Advertiser*, first Irish daily newspaper.

1737
First publication by Francis Joy of *Belfast News-Letter*, Ireland's oldest newspaper still in continuous production.

1738
Death of Turlough O'Carolan, harpist and composer, 25 March.

1739–1740
Severe winter weather from Christmas to February causes acute food shortages and famine.

1740
Bread riots in Dublin as food crisis deepens.

Percentage of households Catholic – 1732	
Leinster	79%
Ulster	38%
Munster	89%
Connacht	91%
Nationally	73%

The Old Library, Trinity College, Dublin, dates from 1712 and is one of the great architectural triumphs of the Irish Georgian period. The ceiling was originally flat: the present magnificent barrel-vaulted ceiling is a Victorian addition.

Ascendancy

For most of the eighteenth century, Ireland was ruled by a tiny Anglican elite – probably no more than 10 per cent of the population: the ascendancy, as they were later known. All *ancien régime* governments were tiny minorities: nowhere in Europe was there any notion of popular sovereignty or majority rule, ideas that for most of human history had been thought synonymous with mob rule and anarchy. Government was the business of property owners. No one else counted as part of the political nation. And no kind of property counted for more than land.

The ascendancy thought of themselves as local grandees governing in the king's name, just as their equivalents did in Northumberland or Bavaria or Languedoc. The difference was that Ireland in theory was a separate kingdom, although sharing a common king with England. At the same time, it was plain that the ascendancy were – as many of them saw themselves – the English in Ireland. Most ascendancy families had been settled in Ireland following the Cromwellian confiscations of Catholic lands in the 1650s. As such, they had many of the qualities of a colonial garrison. The ascendancy was never quite sure what it was. Was it merely the natural ruling class of a separate kingdom? Or a peripheral elite at the margin of a larger Anglo-Irish world? Or a colonial pro-consular bridgehead? There was no unanimous answer to these questions.

Those who thought of themselves as the natural ruling class in a separate kingdom increasingly put the emphasis on that separate constitutional status. Known from the 1770s as the Patriot party, they were influential in parliament and helped secure an increased measure of parliamentary independence in 1782, when they ended the centuries-long practice whereby laws passed in the Irish parliament had to be endorsed at Westminster. Their best-known figure was Henry Grattan. Significantly, most of them – although not Grattan – were opposed to parliamentary reform which would have extended the franchise to some Catholics.

The peripherals, if we may call them that, were best represented by writers like Swift, Sheridan, Goldsmith and Burke, who saw London as the great cultural metropolis towards which they were magnetically drawn by their political and artistic ambition. For them, Ireland and England were parts of a common world united in language, religion and culture with its umbilicus in London, the largest, most populous city in the world.

The colonial governors were the no-nonsense element among the ascendancy. Their best-known figures – John

Fitzgibbon (Lord Clare) and John Beresford – dominated the administration of government along with a succession of London-appointed lords lieutenant. Their bailiwick was not the parliament house on College Green, which they generally despised as a talking shop, but Dublin Castle, from which the king's government in Ireland was actually run. And it was run quite self-consciously with a clear-eyed appreciation of England's strategic interests. Lord Clare, a highly intelligent reactionary in the mould of Metternich, understood the realities. He maintained a constant communication with the London government. He was bitterly opposed to reform which might give Catholics an entrée into the world of influence and power. He saw Ireland's position in simple colonial terms: an English Protestant redoubt athwart the western approaches, whose Catholic majority must be kept remote from power – which meant land ownership and its extension, politics – because they could not be trusted to remain loyal if the French invaded. He was under no illusions about the depth of Catholic grievances and resentments: the burning sense of dispossession arising from the confiscations of the previous century; the hoped-for restoration of the Stuart dynasty with the help of French arms; and the basic illegitimacy of most ascendancy land titles, for as he admitted in one famous speech "the Act by which most of us hold our estates was an Act of violence – an Act subverting the first principles of the common law in England and Ireland".

Silver-gilt mace, the symbol of authority of the old Irish House of Lords. This elegant silver work was made in Dublin around 1760.

In the early eighteenth century, the newly-victorious Protestant interest passed a series of penal laws against Catholics and Dissenters, of which those against the former were more severe. Their purpose was to maintain access to land and power as an Anglican preserve rather than to secure conversions. While they were not enforced rigorously, they none the less had the effect of driving many Ulster Presbyterians into exile in America while reducing the Catholic community to second-class status at best. From the 1760s on, the situation improved: the papal recognition of the Hanoverian monarchy in 1766, and its concomitant abandonment of the Stuart cause, was a key moment. The first Catholic Relief Acts were passed in 1793, although the final disabilities on Catholics were not removed until 1829.

At least, the long ascendancy hegemony brought peace after the turmoil of the seventeenth century. The splendours of Irish Georgian architecure – from great country houses like Castletown to the serene urbanity of Dublin's great squares – are the most enduring legacy of the period.

1741

1741
Famine. Up to 400,000 deaths estimated out of a population of about 2.5 million, a higher proportionate mortality than in the Great Famine of 1845–52.

1742
Handel's *Messiah* given its inaugural performance under the baton of the composer in Dublin, 13 April.

1745
Opening of Dr Bartholomew Mosse's lying-in hospital, later the Rotunda, in Dublin, the first maternity hospital in Britain or Ireland.

1745
Death of Jonathan Swift, 19 October.

1745
Building of Leinster House, Kildare St, Dublin begins. Richard Castle, architect.

1746
Battle of Culloden marks the effective end of any hope of a Stuart restoration in Britain or Ireland.

1747
First of 43 visits to Ireland by John Wesley, the founder of Methodism, the last of which was in 1789.

1752
Change from Julian to Gregorian calendar entails "loss" of eleven days.

1752
First ever steeplechase is run in Co. Cork between horses owned by Messrs Blake and O'Callaghan, from Buttevant church to the steeple of the St Leger Church at Doneraile.

1756
Start of Seven Years' War.

1756
Construction of the Grand Canal begins; continues to 1805.

1757
Opening of St Patrick's Hospital, Dublin, Swift's "home for fools and mad", built with money bequeathed by the Dean in his will.

1757
Act of parliament establishes the Wide Streets Commissioners for the city of Dublin.

1757
First patients admitted to the Rotunda Hospital.

1759
Foundation of brewery at St James's Gate, Dublin by Arthur Guinness.

1759
Completion of west front of TCD (variously attributed to Henry Keene & John Sanderson or to Theodore Jacobsen).

1760
French force under Admiral Francois Thurot occupies Carrickfergus, Co. Antrim, for a week.

1760
Accession of King George III (until 1820).

1760
Catholic Committee founded, the first organised group to press for the relief of Catholic disabilities since the start of the penal era.

1761
First outbreak of agrarian violence by the Whiteboys, a secret society

distinguished by the white shirts worn by their adherents. Focused in Co. Tipperary, their agitation spread to surrounding counties. Their principal grievances concerned the enclosure of common land and the payment of tithes to the clergy of the Church of Ireland.

1763
First publication of *Freeman's Journal*, destined to be one of the most influential nationalist newspapers of the nineteenth century. It survived until 1924.

1766
Death of the Old Pretender (son of James II, father of Bonnie Prince Charlie) leads to papal recognition of the Hanoverian dynasty in Britain.

1766
Fr Nicholas Sheehy hanged in Clonmel, Co. Tipperary, having been convicted by a packed jury on perjured evidence of inciting Whiteboy outrages; regarded then and since as judicial murder.

1768
Octennial Act limits life of each parliament to eight years rather than to the lifetime of the reigning monarch, as previously.

1770
Lord North prime minister.

1771
Benjamin Franklin visits Ireland.

1773
Art Ó Laoghaire shot dead in Co. Cork by persons acting for Abraham Morris, High Sheriff of

Cork; his widow, Eibhlín Dubh Ní Chonaill, composed the Caoineadh Airt Uí Laoghaire (Lament for Art O'Leary), the most famous such poem in the Irish language.

1775

Henry Flood, previously leader of the "Patriot" opposition in the Irish parliament, accepts government office. He is replaced by Henry Grattan.

Castletown House, Co. Kildare, was built in the 1720s for William Conolly, Speaker of the Irish House of Commons, reputedly the richest man in Ireland. Designed by the Florentine architect Alessandro Galilei, the building reflects the prevailing Italianate style and is generally considered to be the finest of all the Irish great houses.

MODERN IRELAND

1778
Gardiner's Catholic Relief Act allows Catholics to take leases for 999 years; first major repeal of penal laws.

1779
Opening of first section of the Grand Canal.

1779
First mass parade of Volunteers in College Green, Dublin in support of Irish demands to trade with British colonies on the same basis as Britain.

1780
First pub. Arthur Young, *A Tour in Ireland*.

1782
Gardiner's second Relief Act allows Catholics to buy land, except in parliamentary boroughs.

1782
Legislative independence means repeal of Poynings'

Volunteers saluting the statue of William III on College Green, Dublin, 4 November 1779.

Law (1494) and Declaratory Act (1720) and a reduction in the formal power of London over Dublin in parliamentary matters, but not in administrative ones.

1783
Foundation of Bank of Ireland.

1785
Foundation of Royal Irish Academy.

1789
Fall of the Bastille marks start of French Revolution.

1791
Foundation of Society of United Irishmen in Belfast.

1791
Opening of Custom House, Dublin (architect, James Gandon).

1792
Catholic convention meets in Tailor's Hall, Dublin (the "Back Lane Parliament").

1793
Britain joins first coalition against revolutionary France; will be at war with

France intermittently until 1815.

1793
Opening of St Patrick's College, Carlow, the first college for the higher education of Catholics in Ireland.

1794
Suppression of Dublin Society of United Irishmen. Wolfe Tone goes abroad.

1795
The liberal Lord Fitzwilliam is appointed lord lieutenant of Ireland, only to be dismissed within two months.

1795
Foundation of Catholic seminary, St Patrick's College, Maynooth, Co. Kildare.

1795
Battle of the Diamond in Co. Armagh between the Protestant "Peep o' Day Boys" and the Catholic Defenders leads the former to regroup as the Orange Order.

A Georgian interior, showing delicate plasterwork and stucco. The extended peace of the eighteenth century, following the upheavals of the previous century and prior to the instability introduced by the influence of the French Revolution, allowed the domestic arts to flourish among the Ascendancy rulers of Ireland.

1796

A meeting of the United Irishmen.

1796
Wolfe Tone in France.

1796
French invasion fleet with 15,000 troops arrives at Bantry Bay, Co. Cork but cannot land due to contrary winds.

1797
Government troops under General Gerard Lake crack down on unrest in the countryside.

1798
Rising by the United Irishmen. The main rising breaks out on 23 May in Leinster, quickly becoming confined to Co. Wexford. Almost 30,000 die before Wexford rising is finally defeated at Vinegar Hill, above Enniscorthy, on 21 June.

1798
An Ulster rising broke out in Cos Antrim and Down on 6 June but rebels are routed by government troops at Ballynahinch a week later. A small French force lands in Connacht on 22 August but surrenders on 8 September. Another French landing in Co. Donegal in October includes Wolfe Tone, who is arrested, tried and convicted of treason but commits suicide rather than hang.

1799
Napoleon takes power in France.

1800
Irish parliament votes to dissolve itself and unite with Westminster.

1801
Act of Union takes effect on New Year's Day, thus creating the United Kingdom of Great Britain and Ireland and introducing the Union Jack flag. Catholic emancipation, which was to have been part of the union settlement, is rejected by King George III. Pitt resigns as prime minister.

1802
Completion of the Four Courts, Dublin (James Gandon, architect).

1803
Robert Emmet's rebellion in Dublin descends into little more than an affray. After a memorable speech from the dock, Emmet executed.

1808
Erection of Nelson Pillar in Sackville (later O'Connell) St, Dublin (until 1966).

1808
Foundation of Christian Brothers by Edmund Ignatius Rice.

1811
Prince of Wales (later George IV) assumes regency because of his father's insanity.

1812
Robert Peel chief secretary of Ireland (until 1818).

1814
Publication of letter from Monsignor Giovanni Quarantotti, secretary of the Congregation of Propaganda Fide in the Vatican, supporting a government veto on the appointment of bishops to the Irish Catholic church in return for Catholic Emancipation. The veto opposed by a majority of Irish Catholic opinion, which demands unconditional emancipation.

1815
Battle of Waterloo finally ends the long series of French Revolutionary wars.

1815
Catholic movement splits over veto issue; pro-veto minority secede; division not healed until the next decade.

1815
First Bianconi car service begins operation between Clonmel and Cahir, Co. Tipperary.

1815
At the site known ever since as Donnelly's Hollow, on the Curragh, Co. Kildare, Irish champion prize fighter Dan Donnelly defeats the English champion, Cooper, in eleven rounds.

1816
Opening of Wellington Bridge over the Liffey in Dublin. Better known as the Metal Bridge and even better known again as the

1829

Ha'penny Bridge, from the toll that was charged to cross it until 1919.

1817

First total abstinence society in Europe formed in Co. Cork.

1817

First ever balloon crossing of the Irish Sea made by William Sadler.

1817

Famine caused by poor potato harvest in 1816. The misery is compounded by a typhus epidemic.

1818

General Post Office, in Sackville (later O'Connell) St, Dublin, opens. Architect, Francis Johnston.

1819

The murder of Ellen Hanley, the *Colleen Bawn*, in Limerick, the inspiration for Gerald Griffin's novel *The Collegians* (1829), Dion Boucicault's play *The Colleen Bawn* (1861) and Jules Benedict's opera *The Lily of Killarney* (1862).

1820

Death of King George III. Prince Regent succeeds as George IV.

1820

Completion of Wellington Monument in Phoenix Park, Dublin, the tallest obelisk in Europe.

1820

Completion of Bull Wall, enclosing the northern end of the approach to Dublin port.

1821

King George IV visits Ireland, the first ever such visit by an English

monarch for a wholly peaceful purpose. He arrives drunk.

1823

Formation of the Catholic association by Daniel O'Connell.

1825

Opening of St Mary's Pro-Cathedral, Dublin, the largest Catholic church erected in the city since the Reformation.

1825

Catholic Association dissolves itself under the terms of the new Unlawful Societies Act; immediately reconstitutes itself as the New Catholic Association.

1825

Sir Francis Burdett MP introduces a Catholic Emancipation bill with "wings" or conditions: the disenfranchisement of forty shilling freeholders and state stipends for Catholic priests. O'Connell supported the bill, which was defeated in the Lords.

1826

Currency union between Britain and Ireland.

1826

General election. Pro-Emancipation candidate in Waterford defeats Lord George Beresford, a member of one of the most powerful ascendancy families, thanks to O'Connell's mobilisation of Catholic voters and their unprecedented revolt against their landlords' instructions.

1827

Opening of the first Sisters of Mercy school in Ireland, at Baggot Street in Dublin.

1828

Clare by-election: although forbidden to take his seat because of his Catholicism, O'Connell fights and wins in contest against William Vesey Fitzgerald.

1828

The so-called "invasion of Ulster", organised by O'Connell's lieutenant John Lawless to spread the Catholic cause to Ulster, is forced to retreat when confronted by armed Orangemen at Ballybay, Co. Monaghan.

1828

Foundation of the Brunswick Clubs, a Tory pressure group.

1828

Nineteen people drown following a boating accident on Lough Corrib near Annaghdown, Co. Galway. The tragedy inspired the poet Raftery to write *Anach Chuain* as a memorial.

1828

Split in Ulster Presbyterianism between Trinitarians under Rev. Henry Cooke and Unitarians under Rev. Henry Montgomery.

1829

Catholic Emancipation abolishes the remaining penal laws. Catholics may now sit in parliament and hold senior judicial and administrative offices hitherto denied to them.

1829

Re-run of Clare by-election following passage of Catholic Emancipation: O'Connell returned unopposed, the first Catholic MP at Westminster since the Reformation.

Nationalism

In Ireland, the French Revolution inspired a wave of radical enthusiasm which the authorities suppressed with military repression, and which led ultimately to something akin to a civil war. From the period of the revolution can be traced the strong element of democratic republican ideals which became part of Irish popular political culture. For the French, Ireland was seen as a weak spot in England's defences and hence they responded favourably to Wolfe Tone's appeals for military assistance by sending an expeditionary force to Ireland in December 1796 under the leadership of General Lazare Hoche.

MODERN IRISH nationalism had two tributary sources. One was the secular republicanism of the French Revolution, the other the sense of Catholic grievance – rooted in the land confiscations of the seventeenth century and the penal laws of the eighteenth. These two traditions within Irish nationalism have co-existed, not always comfortably, since the 1790s.

In the wake of the French Revolution, the Society of United Irishmen was founded in Belfast and Dublin. Its promoters were mainly Protestants disaffected from the regime and caught up in the heady idealism of the French Revolution. Wolfe Tone, a young liberal Anglican lawyer, was the society's best-known figure. The United Irishmen proposed a startlingly new definition of Irishness: that it should be an inclusive union of Catholic, Protestant (Anglican) and Dissenter, in other words that civic loyalty to the nation should transcend all confessional divisions.

Inevitably, the appeal of such a novel doctrine was strongest among young, educated liberals: journalists, lawyers and intellectuals. The movement made impressive progress in spreading its doctrines outside this core constituency, however, so that it acquired the shape of a national movement.

The entry of Britain into the revolutionary wars against France in 1793, however, changed the picture. Bodies like the United Irishmen, with their avowed sympathy for revolutionary France, became a security risk. Tone was arrested in 1794 and forced to emigrate to America, from where he made his way in time to France.

In the meantime, there were other organisations on the ground less idealistic than the United Irishmen. Most prominent of these was an agrarian secret society called the Defenders, concentrated mainly in the north Leinster and south Ulster areas. It was avowedly Catholic. Its purpose was to defend its community against rival Protestant societies, of which the best known became the Orange Order.

The Orange Order was founded in Co. Armagh in 1795 following a sectarian affray. The area of mid-Armagh in which the affray took place had a particularly delicate demographic balance as between Catholics, Anglicans and Dissenters, with consequent rivalries over employment and other matters. The Orange Order, destined to be a populist mobilising force for lower-class Protestants (at first mainly Anglican, later pan-Protestant) was from the first bitterly opposed to Irish nationalism or to anything which in its eyes represented improved conditions for Catholics.

In 1796, the persistent efforts of Wolfe Tone in Paris bore

fruit in the form of a French naval invasion force of 15,000 crack troops under the command of General Lazare Hoche which reached Bantry Bay in West Cork just before Christmas. Frustratingly, it could not land because of contrary winds and limped back to France. Two years later, in 1798, the United Irishmen did organise a rising which ended bloodily in a few weeks. Confined principally to Co. Wexford, it resulted in the death of over 30,000 people – most of them non-combatants – in less than a month. Moreover, the non-sectarian idealism of the United Irishmen was compromised by some sectarian atrocities. These were not definitive of the rising, but they were a reminder that Defenderism, in one form or another, was an older Irish tradition than secular republicanism.

Ireland's status as a separate kingdom did not long survive the trauma of 1798. An Act of Union (1801) created the United Kingdom of Great Britain and Ireland, thus absorbing Ireland wholly into the British metropolitan state for the first time. Ironically, this incorporation came precisely at the time that Irish national consciousness was maturing.

What caused this heightened sense of nationhood? The republican legacy of the United Irishmen; the revival of the Catholic Church, which can be traced to the 1760s; the gradual removal of Catholic disabilities, which facilitated the rise of a Catholic middle class; and a persistent recollection of past grievances. The obvious failure of revolutionary republicanism as a vehicle for further advance left the way open for an older organising principle to supply the motor of nationalism: the solidarity of the catholic communty.

Nationalism found a leader of genius in Daniel O'Connell, a Kerry lawyer. In the 1820s, he organised the first political mass movement in modern European history in support of Catholic Emancipation – the removal of the last Catholic disabilities, including that forbidding them to sit in parliament. With the threat of serious civil disturbance in Ireland staring it in the face, the London government conceded in 1829. It was a seminal moment, the symbolic end of the penal era and a reminder of the hitherto untapped power of Catholic numbers. O'Connell's later campaign for the repeal of the Act of Union was unsuccessful, but his position in Irish history was secure. Henceforth, for better or worse, Irish nationalism would mean the organised political project of the Catholic community. It never completely forgot or neglected the secular republican tradition, but after 1829 it was set on an unambiguously confessional course.

Daniel O'Connell (1775–1847), the nephew and heir of a Catholic landowner in Kerry, first came to note as being one of the few Catholics prominent in opposing the Union in 1800. His skills as a political leader were his oratory, organisational ability and sheer brinkmanship. He effected the junction between Catholicism and nationalism, while enjoying a European reputation as a liberal.

1830

1830
Opening of Dublin Zoo, the second oldest in the world.

1830
Death of King George IV; succeeded by William IV.

1831
Start of tithe war, violent agrarian agitation in opposition to the requirement that tithes be paid for the support of clergy of the Church of Ireland.

1831
Structures established for the development of a system of national education in Ireland.

1832
First publication of *Dublin Penny Journal* and *Dublin University Magazine*.

1832
Parliamentary reform act increases Irish representation at Westminster from 100 to 105 MPs.

1834
St Vincent's Hospital, Dublin opens under the auspices of the Sisters of Charity.

1834
Opening of Dublin & Kingstown Railway, the first line in Ireland.

1835
Lichfield House Compact, in which Daniel O'Connell promises support to the Whigs in return for Irish reforms.

1836
Establishment of the Irish Constabulary (from 1867 the Royal Irish Constabulary) and the Dublin Metropolitan Police.

1837
Death of King William IV; succeeded by Queen Victoria.

1838
Foundation of Fr Theobald Mathew's temperance movement, soon to be the single greatest mass movement in pre-Famine Ireland.

1838
Enactment of the Irish Poor Law.

1838
End of the tithe war: tithes abolished and converted to a rent charge with amounts reduced.

1840
Formation of the General Assembly of the Presbyterian Church in Ireland.

1840
Formation of the Repeal Association under the leadership of O'Connell to agitate for the restoration of the Dublin parliament.

1841
First accurate Irish census shows a population of over 8 million, a figure never attained since.

1841
First publication of the *Cork Examiner*.

1841
Daniel O'Connell elected first Catholic lord mayor of Dublin since 1688.

1842
First publication of *The Nation*.

1843
Monster meetings in support of repeal held at different locations, including many historic

sites, but meeting planned for Clontarf – near Dublin – proscribed by the government, whereupon O'Connell abandons it.

1844
O'Connell convicted of conspiracy and jailed.

1844
The third earl of Rosse constructs the largest telescope in the world in the grounds of Birr Castle, King's County (now Co. Offaly).

1845
First appearance of the potato blight which causes the Great Famine. Little hardship this year: Peel's government puts effective relief measures swiftly in place.

1845
Establishment of Queen's Colleges at Belfast, Cork and Galway: non-denominational universities promptly dubbed "godless colleges" by O'Connell and a majority of the Catholic hierarchy but welcomed by the Young Ireland group close to *The Nation*.

1846
Total failure of the potato harvest. First relief works introduced by act of parliament: over 300,000 people, almost 10 per cent of the entire Irish labour force, employed in relief schemes by year end.

1846
Young Ireland group withdraws from Repeal Association following division on the question of physical force, which Young Ireland refuses to rule out.

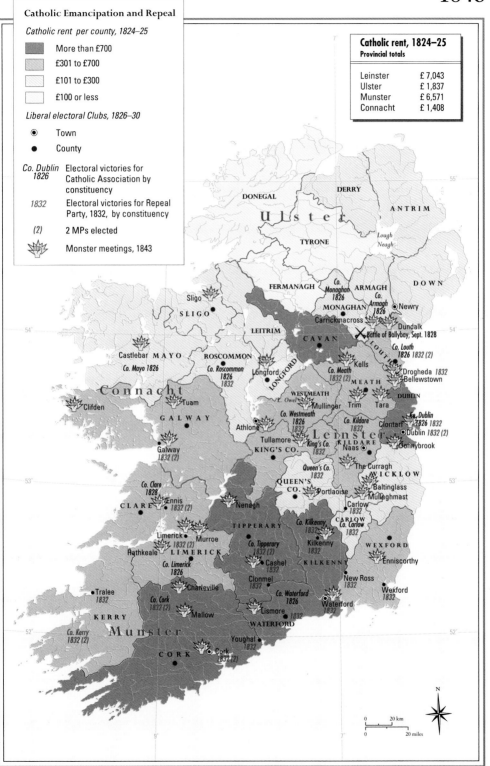

Catholic Emancipation and Repeal

Catholic rent per county, 1824–25

- More than £700
- £301 to £700
- £101 to £300
- £100 or less

Liberal electoral Clubs, 1826–30

- ⦿ Town
- ● County

Co. Dublin
1826 — Electoral victories for Catholic Association by constituency

1832 — Electoral victories for Repeal Party, 1832, by constituency

(2) — 2 MPs elected

— Monster meetings, 1843

Catholic rent, 1824–25 Provincial totals	
Leinster	£ 7,043
Ulster	£ 1,837
Munster	£ 6,571
Connacht	£ 1,408

DONEGAL

DERRY

Ulster

ANTRIM

TYRONE

Lough Neagh

FERMANAGH

Co. Monaghan 1826

ARMAGH

Co. Armagh 1826

DOWN

Sligo

MONAGHAN

● Newry

SLIGO

Carrickmacross

Dundalk

Battle of Ballybay, Sept. 1828

LEITRIM

CAVAN

Co. Louth 1826 1832 (2)

Castlebar MAYO

ROSCOMMON

Kells

Drogheda 1832

Co. Mayo 1826

Co. Roscommon 1826 1832

Longford

Co. Meath 1832 (2)

MEATH

Bellewstown

Connacht

Clifden

Tuam

WESTMEATH

L. Owel

Mullingar

Trim

Tara

DUBLIN

GALWAY

Athlone

Co. Westmeath 1826

Co. Kildare 1832

Clontarf

Co. Dublin 1826 1832

Galway 1832 (2)

Tullamore

King's Co. 1832

Leinster

KILDARE

Dublin 1832 (2)

Donnybrook

KING'S CO.

Naas ⦿

Co. Clare 1828

Queen's Co. 1832

QUEEN'S CO.

The Curragh

WICKLOW

CLARE

Ennis 1832 (2)

Nenagh

Portlaoise

Baltinglass

Mullaghmast

Carlow 1832

Limerick 1832 (2)

Murroe

TIPPERARY

Co. Kilkenny 1832

CARLOW

Co. Carlow 1832

Rathkeale

LIMERICK

Co. Tipperary 1832 (2)

Kilkenny 1832

WEXFORD

Co. Limerick 1826

Cashel 1832

KILKENNY

Enniscorthy

Tralee 1832

Charleville

Clonmel 1832

New Ross 1832

Co. Cork 1832 (2)

Mallow

Co. Waterford 1826

Wexford 1832

KERRY

Lismore

Waterford 1832

Co. Kerry 1832 (2)

Munster

WATERFORD

Youghal 1832

CORK

Cork 1832 (2)

N

0   20 km

0   20 miles

1847

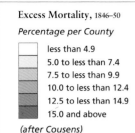

Excess Mortality, 1846–50

Percentage per County

	less than 4.9
	5.0 to less than 7.4
	7.5 to less than 9.9
	10.0 to less than 12.4
	12.5 to less than 14.9
	15.0 and above

(after Cousens)

1847
Exchequer ends central provision of relief funds, which are henceforth to be met from local rates in each locality.

1847
Irish Confederation formed by Young Ireland dissenters from Repeal Association under William Smith O'Brien. Relations between the two groups break down.

1847
Death of Daniel O'Connell.

1847
Black '47: the worst year of the Famine. The total failure of the previous harvest meant fewer seed potatoes to plant and therefore a reduced harvest this year. Ironically, it was free of blight. Number of total deaths in Ireland more than double that for 1846.

1848
First appearance of the green, white and orange tricolour flag, brought back to the Irish Confederation from Paris by Thomas Francis Meagher. A conscious copy of the French republican tricolour, it will become the national flag of the Irish Free State/Republic of Ireland from 1922.

1848
Another catastrophic failure of the potato harvest, as in 1846.

1848
John Mitchel and radical faction secede from Irish Confederation and publish first issue of the *United Irishman*.

1848
Treason Felony Act passed. Mitchel first to be tried and convicted under its terms; he is sentenced to transportation for fourteen years.

1848
Over 833,000 people in receipt of outdoor relief.

1848
Affray at Ballingarry, Co. Tipperary when police attempt to arrest William Smith O'Brien. O'Brien and Meagher later convicted of high treason and sentenced to death, commuted to transportation in both cases.

1849
Affray at Dolly's Brae, Co. Down in which Orangemen overwhelm Ribbonmen: celebrated afterwards in Orange ballad.

1849
Encumbered Estates Act passed to facilitate the sale of estates ruined by the Famine, so that they can be carried on by solvent owners.

Total Numbers in Workhouses, 1844–53 (after Nicholls)		
Year	Number of Workhouses in Operation	Total No. of Persons Relieved During the Year
1844	113	105,358
1845	123	114,205
1846	130	243,933
1847	130	417,139
1848	131	610,463
1849	131	932,284
1850	163	805,702
1851	163	707,443
1852	163	504,864
1853	163	396,438

1850

Paul Cullen appointed archbishop of Armagh.

1850

Opening of Synod of Thurles, first meeting of the Catholic bishops of Ireland since the seventeenth century. Its decrees deepen the movement to liturgical orthodoxy and ultramontanism in the Irish church.

1851

Group of Irish MPs form themselves into the Catholic Defence Association, disparagingly known as the Pope's Brass Band.

1852

Paul Cullen Catholic archbishop of Dublin in succession to Daniel Murray.

1853

John Mitchel escapes from Van Diemen's Land and makes his way to the United States.

1853

Irish Industrial Exhibition held in Dublin; visited by Queen Victoria.

1854

Establishment of Catholic University in Dublin, lineal antecedent of UCD. John Henry Newman first rector.

1854

Donnybrook Fair takes place for the last time; subsequently suppressed by the authorities because of public disorder associated with it, thus giving the word "donnybrook" to the language.

1857

Severe rioting in Belfast following Orange celebration on 12 July.

1858

Establishment of the IRB/Fenian Brotherhood simultaneously in Ireland and the United States.

This illustration taken from The Illustrated London News *in 1849 shows Bridget O'Donnell and her children. One of the few images published showing true emaciation.*

1859

First publication of *The Irish Times*.

1860

Over £80,000 collected nationwide at Catholic churches to support Papal States in their resistance to

1860

the Italian Risorgimento. Irish battalion fights for the Pope.

1860

Deasy's Act states that landlord and tenant relationships are grounded in contract law alone and not in tenure or service. It is the last legislative endorsement of this traditional view prior to Gladstone's Land Acts.

1861

Opening of Mater Hospital, Dublin.

1861

Funeral of Terence Bellew McManus, Young Irelander, in Dublin a major *coup de theatre* by the Fenians. Largest funeral in the city since O'Connell's.

1862

Foundation of Harland & Wolff shipyard, Belfast.

1863

First publication of *The Irish People*, a Fenian paper.

1864

Opening of the National Gallery of Ireland.

1864

Laying of foundation stone for O'Connell Monument, Dublin.

1865

Police raids close the offices of *The Irish People*; leading Fenians arrested, but James Stephens escapes and flees to France. Long sentences for others, including John O'Leary, Thomas Clarke Luby and Jeremiah O'Donovan Rossa.

1866

Suspension of habeas corpus (February).

1866

Fenian troops in the United States cross the Canadian border and occupy Fort Erie, which they hold for three days.

1866

Paul Cullen, archbishop of Dublin, first Irish cardinal.

1867

Fenian rising. Minor outbreaks in various locations, but the rebels' plans betrayed to the police by informers. The police acquire the "Royal" prefix for their part in containing the Fenians, becoming the Royal Irish Constabulary.

1867

A rescue of Fenian prisoners in Manchester results in the death of a policeman and the conviction and execution of William Allen, Michael Larkin and Michael O'Brien, the "Manchester Martyrs". In their memory, T.D. Sullivan writes "God Save Ireland", the anthem of nationalist Ireland for the next fifty years.

1867

Fenian bomb in Clerkenwell, London, kills seventeen people and injures over a hundred.

1868

Foundation of Irish National Teachers' Organisation.

1868

Gladstone prime minister.

1869

Act of parliament to disestablish the Church of Ireland (takes effect 1871).

1870

Home Government Association founded by

Isaac Butt to campaign for Irish home rule.

1870

Gladstone's First Land Act, the first attempt to give statutory protection to tenants.

1872

Severe sectarian rioting in Belfast.

1874

General election returns 59 Irish Home Rule MPs, pledged to parliamentary independence. Disraeli prime minister. First use of obstruction in House of Commons by radical home rulers, although disapproved of by Butt.

1875

Charles Stewart Parnell elected MP for Co. Meath.

1876

Establishment of the "Skirmishing Fund" in New York by O'Donovan Rossa, to finance Fenian attacks on Britain.

1876

The Supreme Council of the Irish Republican Brotherhood (otherwise the Fenians) withdraws support previously offered to the Home Rule party and orders Fenians in the party to withdraw.

1877

Parnell replaces Butt as president of the Home Rule Confederation of Great Britain.

1877

Michael Davitt released from prison after seven years for Fenian activities.

1878

Murder of Lord Leitrim, a notoriously severe landlord, in Co. Donegal.

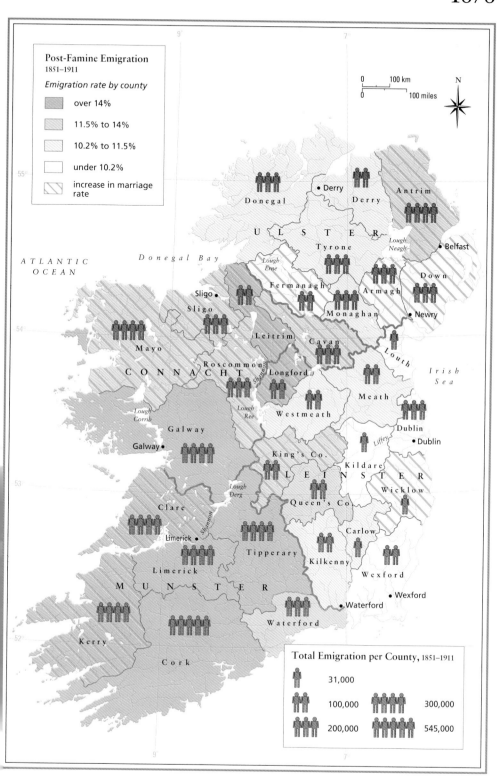

Post-Famine Emigration
1851–1911

Emigration rate by county

- over 14%
- 11.5% to 14%
- 10.2% to 11.5%
- under 10.2%
- increase in marriage rate

ATLANTIC
OCEAN

ULSTER

Donegal Bay

Lough
Erne

Lough
Neagh

CONNACHT

Sligo

Mayo

Roscommon

Galway

Lough
Corrib

Lough
Ree

Lough
Derg

Shannon

Clare

Limerick

Limerick

MUNSTER

Kerry

Cork

Derry

Derry

Donegal

Tyrone

Fermanagh

Monaghan

Armagh

Antrim

Belfast

Down

Newry

Leitrim

Cavan

Louth

Longford

Westmeath

Meath

Dublin

Dublin

King's Co.

Kildare

LEINSTER

Wicklow

Queen's Co.

Tipperary

Carlow

Kilkenny

Wexford

Waterford

Wexford

Waterford

Irish
Sea

Liffey

Total Emigration per County, 1851–1911

- 31,000
- 100,000
- 200,000
- 300,000
- 545,000

1878

The Catholic revival in stone. University Church in St Stephen's Green, Dublin, dates from the 1850s.
The college chapel of the newly-formed Catholic University (the antecedent of the present UCD), its
exuberant neo-Byzantine interior was intended as a deliberate contrast to the low-church austerity of
Irish Protestant architecture.

1878

Death of Cardinal Cullen.

1878

Davitt in New York agrees a policy with John Devoy of Clan na Gael known as the New Departure, whereby republicans, constitutionalists and agrarian radicals undertake to co-operate.

1879

Foundation of Irish National Land League in Dublin by Davitt and Parnell, following successful resistance in Co. Mayo to proposed rent increases during agricultural depression

compounded by exceptionally bad weather.

1879

Marian apparitions reported at Knock, Co. Mayo, later to become Ireland's premier Marian shrine.

1880

General election returns Gladstone to power. Parnell elected chairman of Home Rule parliamentary party.

1880

Parnell calls for obedience to the disciplines of the Land League and proposes that those who defy them should be sent to "a moral Coventry". The first victim

is a land agent in Co. Mayo, Captain Boycott, whose name thus enters the language.

1880

Parnell arrested and charged with criminal conspiracy to withhold the payment of rents by tenants.

1880

St Stephen's Green, Dublin, opened as a public park.

1881

Gladstone's Second Land Act legalises the "Three Fs" – fair rent, fixity of tenure and free sale – key Land League demands. But Parnell and his supporters oppose it, seeking even more radical measures.

1881

New Coercion Act in response to growing agrarian violence. Parnell and other leading home rulers arrested. Land League outlawed. Issuing of a No-Rent manifesto.

1882

"Kilmainham Treaty" between Parnell and Gladstone secures Parnell's release from prison and an end to the radical phase of the Land War in return for government assistance in the settlement of rent arrears.

1882

Four days later, the Phoenix Park murders: a radical Fenian group called the Invincibles kill Lord Frederick Cavendish, the chief secretary, and Thomas Burke, the under secretary, near the Vice-Regal Lodge in the Phoenix Park, Dublin.

1882

The Catholic University is renamed University College and passes under the direction of the Society of Jesus.

1883

Arrest and conviction of Thomas J. Clarke and others in Britain on a charge of conspiracy to cause dynamite explosions. Sentenced to life imprisonment, Clarke serves fifteen years.

1883

Execution of five Invincibles for the Phoenix Park murders.

1884

Foundation of Gaelic Athletic Association in Thurles, Co. Tipperary.

1884

Representation of the People Act more than trebles the size of the Irish electorate.

1885

Ashbourne Land Act

creates mechanism to advance loans to tenants to purchase their holdings and empowers the Land Commission to purchase entire estates for re-sale.

1885

Formation of the Irish Loyal and Patriotic Union to oppose home rule.

A complex character, the British Prime Minister William Ewart Gladstone (1809–98) developed an interest in Ireland for a number of reasons: one was a sense of moral responsibility, another a genuine belief that Ireland was a separate nation which needed distinct treatment, and a third a conviction that the preservation of the United Kingdom depended on constitutional reform.

1885

THE LAND WAR!
NO RENT!
NO LANDLORDS GRASSLAND

Tenant Farmers, now is the time. Now is the hour.
You proved false to the first call made upon you.
REDEEM YOUR CHARACTER NOW.

NO RENT
UNTIL THE SUSPECTS ARE RELEASED.

The man who pays Rent (whether an abatement
is offered or not) while PARNELL, DILLON &c.,
are in Jail, will be looked upon as a Traitor to his
Country and a disgrace to his class.
No RENT, No Compromise, No Land-
lords' Grassland,
Under any circumstances.
Avoid the Police, and listen not to spying and delu-
ding Bailiffs.
NO RENT! LET THE LANDTHIEVES DO THEIR WORST!

THE LAND FOR THE PEOPLE!

*The Land War, in origin a
campaign of agrarian protest,
succeeded in developing a
rhetoric which challenged the
legitimacy of the very system
of landlordism in Ireland and
equating it with the British
connection. It became a
massive nationalist
mobilisation which provided
the basis for Parnell's political
triumphs.*

1885

General election.
Gladstone declines to
commit to home rule for
Ireland. Parnell calls on
Irish in Britain to vote
Conservative. The result
gives Parnell the balance of
power. Gladstone
announces his conversion
to the home rule cause.

1886

Pro-union demonstration
in Belfast addressed by
Lord Randolph Churchill
who tells his audience that
"Ulster will fight and
Ulster will be right". Severe

sectarian rioting in the city
during the summer.

1886

Introduction of the first
Home Rule bill. It splits the
Liberals, fails in the
Commons by 30 votes, and
results in another general
election which returns a
Conservative government
under Lord Salisbury.

1886

Launch of the Plan of
Campaign, a renewal of
agrarian agitation under
the direction of William
O'Brien and other home
rulers, although with little
support from Parnell. It
entailed the offering of a
"fair rent", failing
acceptance of which the
rent would be withheld
altogether. The campaign
lasted until 1890 and was
not very successful.

1887

The Times publishes article
"Parnellism and Crime",
accusing Parnell of
complicity in the Phoenix
Park murders.

1887

"Mitchelstown massacre".
A meeting in support of
the Plan of Campaign at
Michelstown, Co. Cork is
broken up by the RIC, who
shoot three people dead.

1888

The Vatican condemns the
Plan of Campaign, as does
Parnell, but many of his
senior lieutenants reject the
Vatican intervention and
reiterate their support for
the Plan.

1888

Special Commission
established to look into the
charges made against
Parnell by *The Times*.

1889

At the Special Commission,
a journalist, Richard
Pigott, the source of the
information behind the
"Parnellism and Crime"
articles, is exposed as the
forger of letters allegedly
written by Parnell, who
emerges triumphant and
vindicated. Pigott commits
suicide.

1890

Divorce action of Capt.
William O'Shea, home rule
MP for Galway, against his
wife Katharine, names
Parnell as co-respondent.
The action is not
contested.

1890

Gladstone, under pressure
from evangelical
Protestants in his party,
withdraws support for
Parnell following the
divorce. This splits the Irish
party, which ousts Parnell
from the leadership after a
meeting of unprecedented
bitterness by 44 to 28.

1890

Opening of the National
Library and the National
Museum in Dublin.

1891

Anti-Parnellites defeat
Parnellites in three vicious
by-election campaigns.

1891

Sudden death of Parnell,
aged 45, in October.

1892

Gladstone prime minister
for the fourth time at the
age of 84.

1892

Douglas Hyde delivers his
inaugural presidential
address to the newly-
formed National Literary
Society "On the necessity

of de-anglicising the Irish people".

1893

Second Home Rule bill passes Commons, defeated in Lords.

1893

Over 100,000 unionists protest against home rule in Belfast.

1893

Foundation of the Gaelic League, with the ambition to revive the Irish language as a written and spoken vernacular.

1895

Conviction and imprisonment of Oscar Wilde.

1895

Foundation of Irish Agricultural Organisation Society, a central body for agricultural co-operatives, under the presidency of Sir Horace Plunkett.

1896

Formation of Irish Socialist Republican Party by James Connolly.

1897

First Oireachtas and Feis Ceoil, respectively literary and musical festivals, important moments in the cultural revival.

1898

Centenary of the 1798 rising an opportunity for the expression of widespread Fenian sentiment.

1898

Local Government Act democratises local administration in Ireland and establishes modern system of county councils and urban councils.

1898

Foundation of United Irish League by William O'Brien; aims to break up large grazing farms and the creation of smaller family farms.

1899

Opening of Irish Literary Theatre with productions of W.B. Yeats's *The Countess Cathleen* and Edward Martyn's *The Heather Field*.

1899

Foundation of the Catholic Truth Society of Ireland.

1899

Establishment of the Department of Agriculture and Technical Instruction.

1900

Irish Party re-unites almost ten years after the Parnell split: John Redmond, head of the minority Parnellite faction, elected leader of the reunited party.

1900

Final visit of Queen Victoria to Ireland.

1901

Death of Queen Victoria.

1901

Irish Literary Theatre produces *Casadh an tSúgáin* (*The Twisting of the Rope*) by Douglas Hyde, the first Irish-language play to receive a professional production.

1902

C.S Wyndham chief secretary, with the energetic Sir Antony MacDonnell as under secretary.

1902

A landlord, Capt. John Shawe-Taylor, writes to *The Times* proposing a land conference to settle

Charles Stewart Parnell (1846–91) established his political power through leadership of the Land War, and by portraying an image of himself that appealed to both moderates and extremists alike. His great achievement was in obtaining land reform, especially the 1881 Land Act, and bringing Irish Home Rule to the centre of British politics through a disciplined and independent parliamentary party and a pragmatic alliance with Gladstonian Liberalism.

1903

the issue definitively. The conference meets towards the end of the year.

1903

Land conference recommends tenant purchase with loans advanced by the Treasury in London. The proposal forms the basis for the Irish Land Act 1903, forever known as the Wyndham Act after its sponsor, which effectively solves the land question and creates the modern pattern of family farms.

1903

St Patrick's Day (17 March) a public holiday for the first time.

1903

National speed limit of 20 mph imposed on cars, as red flag requirement is abolished.

1904

Publication of series of articles by Arthur Griffith under the title "The Resurrection of Hungary", proposing a dual monarch solution for the Irish Question along the lines of the Austro-Hungarian settlement of 1967.

1904

Attacks on Jews in Limerick following anti-Semitic incitement in sermons by Fr John Creagh, a local Redemptorist.

1904

Devolution proposal floated by Sir Antony MacDonnell repudiated by Wyndham, who none the less is forced to resign as chief secretary.

1904

Opening of the Abbey Theatre.

1905

Formation of the Ulster Unionist Council to focus the opposition of the province's Protestants to devolution and home rule.

1905

Foundation of Sinn Fein in Dublin by journalist Arthur Griffith.

1906

Liberal landslide in general election. Sir Henry Campbell-Bannerman, a supporter of home rule, prime minister.

1907

First performance of Synge's *Playboy of the Western World* provokes riots at the Abbey.

1907

James Larkin arrives in Belfast to organise local branch of the National Union of Dock Labourers: leads dock strike within months and troops have to replace mutinous police to quell crowd trouble. Larkin also establishes NUDL branch in Dublin.

1907

Theft of so-called Irish Crown Jewels – actually the regalia of the Order of St Patrick – from Dublin Castle. They were never recovered.

1908

Asquith succeeds Campbell-Bannerman as Liberal leader and prime minister.

1908

Irish Universities Act leads to formation of the National University of Ireland and effectively settles the demand for a Catholic university with degree-awarding powers.

1908

Patrick Pearse opens St Enda's boys' school in Dublin with a Gaelic and patriotic ethos and a liberal educational philosophy.

1909

Formation of the Irish Transport and General Workers' Union (now SIPTU) by James Larkin, a key moment in Irish labour history. The ITGWU seeks to organise unskilled as well as skilled workers.

1910

General election returns Liberals once more, but this time dependent on Irish Party support to command a secure majority. Redmond extracts promise of Home Rule bill as price of support.

1910

Edward Carson leader of Irish Unionist MPs.

1910

Death of King Edward VII, succeeded by George V. The Abbey Theatre declines to close in memory of the deceased king, causing it to lose the subsidy of a wealthy English benefactress.

1911

Parliament Act removes the House of Lords' veto, replacing it with a mere power to delay legislation for two years. This has the effect of clearing a major obstacle from the path of home rule.

1912

Sinking of the Titanic, built by Harland & Wolff in Belfast, on her maiden voyage to New York.

1912

Introduction of third
Home Rule bill in House of
Commons.

1912

Ulster Solemn League and

Covenant signed by almost
a quarter of a million men,
some in their own blood,
pledging opposition to
home rule. A similar pledge
was later signed by women.

*Illuminated Address presented
to Douglas Hyde by a New
York branch of Conradh na
Gaeilge on 26 November 1905.
This document was designed
by Éoin A. Ua Liaigh.*

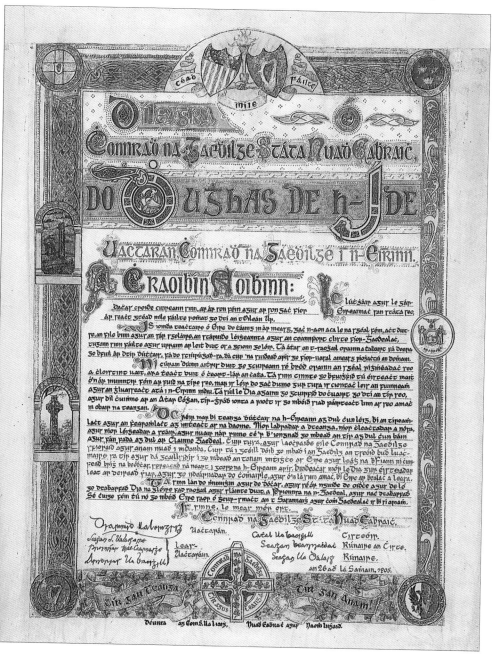

Revolution

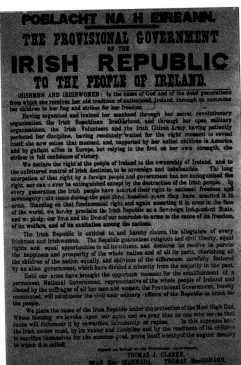

THE GREAT FAMINE of 1845-52 was the last major subsistence crisis in European history. Successive failures of the potato crop brought the deaths of about a million people and the forced emigration of a similar number. The London government saw a providential opportunity to reform the antique structures of the Irish land system and its response to the crisis was rooted in ideology, parsimony and hubris: every quality except humanity. It ensured the lasting hatred of Irish emigrant communities – especially those in the United States – for future British governments.

Nationalism began its revival with the foundation of the Irish Republican Brotherhood in 1858. The IRB (or Fenians, as they were better known) was an insurrectionary secret society, drawing inspiration from 1798 and from contemporary European revolutionary movements. It had no time for politics and aimed to establish an Irish republic by force of arms. An unsuccessful rising in 1867 seemed to knock the stuffing out of the Fenians, however, and opened the way for the return of parliamentary politics.

In the 1880s, Charles Stewart Parnell, an Anglo-Irish landlord from Co. Wicklow, was the unlikely figure who forged an Irish Parliamentary Party that successfully brought the demand for home rule – repeal of the union – to the floor of the House of Commons. It failed, but it secured the support of Gladstone, the greatest of late Victorian prime ministers. Parnell forced the Irish Question onto the British political agenda, where it has remained more or less ever since.

One of the most famous documents in Irish history, the 1916 Proclamation was written largely by Patrick Pearse and approved by the Military Council of the IRB. 2,500 copies were printed in Liberty Hall early on Easter Sunday morning for circulation throughout the country.

Parnell was a master of ambiguity. Although a Protestant, he secured the support of the Catholic hierarchy by endorsing their demands for denominational education; he flirted with (and may even have been a member of) the Fenians; he coupled the question of land reform with the national question and secured a succession of tenant relief acts. Indeed, his success in this area began the movement towards tenant purchase that finally undid the Cromwellian land settlement in 1903, with the break-up of the estates and the establishment of a national network of family farms.

Parnell fell from power following a divorce scandal in which he was named as co-respondent. He died suddenly, aged only 45, in 1891. Politics atrophied for a generation. The Parliamentary Party split, pro- and anti-Parnell. In 1900, the reunited party under John Redmond began to pick up the pieces and by the outbreak of World War I had secured the passage of a Home Rule Act, but it was suspended for the duration of the war. The Act had been passed only in the teeth of ferocious opposition from Protestant Ulster, terrified of being cast into a Catholic nationalist state. It is possible that the outbreak of the European War averted an Irish sectarian civil war.

This was the high-water mark of parliamentary nationalism. The Fenians, meanwhile, small in number, had lost none of their enthusiasm for revolution. A tiny minority of their members – the most ruthless and uncompromising element among nationalists – formed themselves into a secret military council and determined on a rising.

The Easter Rising of 1916 was the work of these men. It lasted for less than a week and was effectively confined to Dublin. Large parts of the city centre were destroyed by British artillery. The leaders were executed. At first public sympathy was withheld from the rebels, but gradually a grudging admiration came to dominate nationalist reaction. A new political party, Sinn Fein (ourselves) began to challenge the Parliamentary Party for the nationalist vote, appealing to the memory of the 1916 martyrs. Sinn Fein swept the boards in nationalist Ireland in the 1918 general election.

Instead of taking their seats at Westminster, the Sinn Fein MPs formed themselves into Dail Eireann (the assembly of Ireland) which met for the first time in January 1919. On the same day, the first shots were fired by the Irish Republican Army (IRA), as the armed wing of the movement now styled itself, in the Irish war of independence. A sporadic affair, it none the less broke the morale of the Royal Irish Constabulary and provoked shameful British reprisals. There was shame on both sides: the IRA was a sectarian as well as a national vehicle.

The war ended in a truce in 1921. In the meantime, the island had been partitioned. The six counties of the northeast were retained in the United Kingdom in deference to their Protestant majority. Negotiations now began between Sinn Fein delegates and the British government regarding the constitutional status of the other twenty-six counties. A treaty was concluded granting dominion status – effective independence but not a republic. The terms of this settlement provoked a civil war in which the pro-Treaty forces quickly triumphed. The Irish Free State, formally established on 6 December 1922, finally broke the link with the British crown which went back to 1177.

1913

1913
Home Rule bill passes
Commons; defeated in
Lords.

1913
Formation of Ulster
Volunteer Force in Belfast
in January to oppose home
rule and of the Irish
Volunteers in Dublin in
November to support it
and nationalist causes
generally. Irish Citizen
Army also formed in
Dublin as trade union
militia.

1913
Dublin lockout, the
greatest labour dispute in
Irish history. Transport
workers, members of
Larkin's ITGWU, were
threatened with the loss of
their jobs if they did not
leave the union. They
refused. Larkin called out
other trades in sympathetic
strikes and paralysed the
city. The employers won by
attrition.

1914
Curragh Mutiny, in which
British army officers
stationed at the Curragh,
Co. Kildare, make it clear
that they will accept
dismissal rather than
enforce home rule on Ulster.

1914
Larne Gun Running. The
UVF successfully land
weapons at Larne, Co.
Antrim.

1914
Buckingham Palace
Conference fails to find
compromise or
accommodation between
nationalists and unionists
in Ireland.

1914
Irish Volunteers land arms

at Howth, Co. Dublin.
Three people later shot
dead by military in city
centre.

1914
Outbreak of the Great War
convulses Europe. Home
rule is suspended until the
end of the war.

1914
Redmond calls for the Irish
Volunteers to support the
British war effort. This
causes a split: a minority
opposed to the war retain
the original name. The
Redmondite majority is
renamed the National
Volunteers.

1914
Formation of 36th (Ulster)
Division from UVF and
16th (Irish) Division largely
from National Volunteers.

1915
Sinking of the Lusitania off
the Old Head of Kinsale
results in the deaths of
1,198 people.

1915
Radical nationalists take
control of the Gaelic
League.

1915
Patrick Pearse delivers
stunning funeral oration at
the grave of Fenian veteran
Jeremiah O'Donovan
Rossa.

1915
Ultra-militant elements
within the IRB organise
themselves as a Military
Council and plot to use the
structures of the Irish
Volunteers as a means to
foment a rising before the
end of the Great War.

1916
Military Council co-opts
James Connolly's Citizen

Army as part of its plans
for a rising.

1916
Arms for the rising arrive
in Tralee Bay, Co. Kerry
from Germany but are
intercepted by a Royal
Navy patrol. Sir Roger
Casement, the procurer of
the arms, is later put
ashore from a U-boat,
arrested and later hanged
in London for high
treason.

1916
Despite this
disappointment, the
Military Council decides to
press ahead with a rising
planned to take place on
Easter Sunday under the
guise of routine Volunteer
manoeuvres. The chief of
staff of the Irish
Volunteers, Eoin Mac
Neill, realising that he has
been deceived by the
Military Council, cancels
the manoeuvres.

1916
The Military Council go
ahead anyway, but now a
day late. On 24 April,
Easter Monday, they
occupy the GPO and a
number of other prominent
buildings across the city of
Dublin. A proclamation of
the Irish Republic is
printed and read out by
Pearse from the steps of the
GPO. There is no rising
outside the city.

1916
After a week, the
insurgents are forced to
surrender, once the British
use artillery against them
and leave much of
O'Connell Street in ruins.
The seven signatories of
the Proclamation of the
Republic, together with
eight other senior rebel

1916

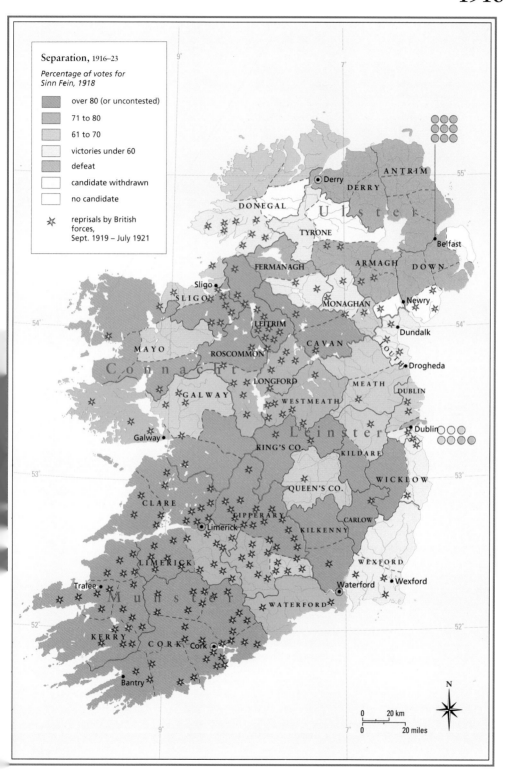

Separation, 1916–23

*Percentage of votes for
Sinn Fein, 1918*

- over 80 (or uncontested)
- 71 to 80
- 61 to 70
- victories under 60
- defeat
- candidate withdrawn
- no candidate
- ✳ reprisals by British forces, Sept. 1919 – July 1921

1916

Roger Casement is pictured aboard a German submarine. The role of the 1916 rebels in seeking German support, in particular the secret shipment to Ireland of German arms, was, in the eyes of the British government at war with Germany, the most serious indictment of their actions.

officers, are shot following courts-martial. They include Tom Clarke, the Pearse brothers and James Connolly.

1916

Battle of the Somme: the 36th (Ulster) Division takes horrific losses on the first day.

1916

Formation of Anti-Partition League as fears rise of a partition settlement of the Irish question at the end of the war.

1917

Sinn Fein become political legatee of the Easter Rising, although it had nothing to do with it. Party re-forms itself as political arm of militant nationalism, in opposition to the Irish Party of Redmond which holds to the constitutional path. Arthur Griffith stands aside from the leadership of Sinn Fein in favour of Eamon de Valera, the most senior surviving Volunteer officer of the Rising.

1917

James Noble, Count Plunkett, the father of Joseph Plunkett – one of those executed following the Easter Rising – wins by-election in North Roscommon against the Irish Party. In line with Sinn Fein policy, he declines to take his seat at Westminster, being pledged to the establishment of an assembly in Ireland. Three more Sinn Fein victories follow in later by-elections – including de Valera's success in Clare – as the Home Rule party's decline continues.

1917

Death of Thomas Ashe, republican, on hunger strike.

1918

Extension of the franchise to all men over 21 and all women over 30 hugely increases the size of the Irish electorate.

1918

Death of John Redmond; succeeded as Home Rule leader by John Dillon.

1918

Proposal to extend conscription to Ireland precipitates withdrawal of Home Rule party from House of Commons and unites all shades of Irish nationalist opinion in opposition. The proposal is later withdrawn.

1918

The so-called "German Plot" – a government fiction – leads to the arrest of Sinn Fein leaders on spurious charges of "treasonable communication with the German enemy".

1918

Martial law declared in large areas of the south and west. Sinn Fein, the Volunteers and most nationalist organisations proscribed.

1918

Armistice ends World War I. The subsequent general election sees Sinn Fein supplant the Home Rulers as the voice of nationalist Ireland.

1919

Rather than take their seats at Westminster, the newly-elected Sinn Fein representatives constitute themselves as Dail Eireann (the assembly of Ireland) in Dublin, adopt a declaration of independence and a constitution.

1919

First shots fired in the war of independence. Two RIC constables are killed in ambush at Soloheadbeg, Co. Tipperary. Widespread incidents of violence occur throughout the country during the year.

1919

Eamon de Valera, who had been held in Lincoln prison in England, escapes. Elected President of the Dail, he sails for New York where he is to spend the next year and a half.

1919

The Dail establishes a system of courts as rivals to crown courts, which are widely used as the means of resolving land disputes and other matters.

1920

Arrival of the Black and Tans and the Auxiliaries to augment depleted and demoralised RIC. By now the Irish Volunteers are styling themselves the Irish Republican Army (IRA).

1920

War continues. Many IRA attacks on RIC personnel around the country, answered by Black and Tan reprisals, which include the assassination of Thomas MacCurtain, mayor of Cork and widespread destruction in the town of Balbriggan, Co. Dublin.

1920

Major sectarian violence in Belfast and other parts of the north. Nineteen killed in Derry in July. Twenty-three people die in Belfast in September alone.

1920

Government of Ireland Act partitions the island, creating two states – Southern Ireland, which never comes into existence in the form intended in the act – and Northern Ireland, comprising the six north-eastern counties of Ulster, in effect the largest county area consistent with a secure Protestant/unionist majority. Thus unionist Northern Ireland secures a form of home rule, while nationalist Southern Ireland rejects it in favour of the more radical demands of Sinn Fein.

1920

Death in prison by hunger strike of Terence MacSwiney, MacCurtain's successor as lord mayor of Cork.

1920

Bloody Sunday, the most violent day of the war of independence. An IRA assassination squad, under the direction of Michael Collins – director of intelligence of the IRA and Minister for Finance in the Dail administration – kills 14 British secret agents in Dublin. In reprisal, three IRA prisoners are shot in cold blood in Dublin Castle and the Black and Tans kill a player and eleven spectators at a Gaelic football match in Croke Park, Dublin.

1920

IRA ambush at Kilmichael, Co. Cork, leaves 18 Auxiliaries dead. Subsequent ambush in Cork leads to Auxiliaries and Black and Tans running amok in the city centre, much of which was destroyed by fire.

1920

De Valera return to Ireland just before Christmas.

1921

Government supports official policy of reprisals against civilian property for IRA attacks. Six republican prisoners executed in Cork; six British soldiers killed in reprisal incidents; mayor of Limerick murdered in his house.

1921

James Craig succeeds Edward Carson as leader of the Ulster Unionists.

1921

Meeting between de Valera and Craig proves fruitless.

1921

First Northern Ireland general election unsurprisingly results in Unionists taking 40 of the 52 seats. Craig appointed first prime minister of the province. King George V

1921

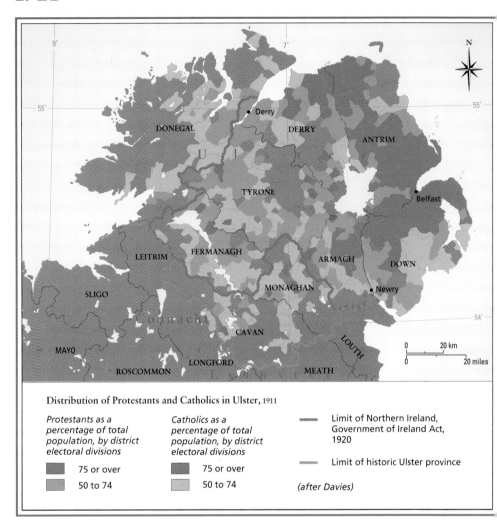

Distribution of Protestants and Catholics in Ulster, 1911

Protestants as a
percentage of total
population, by district
electoral divisions

- 75 or over
- 50 to 74

Catholics as a
percentage of total
population, by district
electoral divisions

- 75 or over
- 50 to 74

—— Limit of Northern Ireland,
Government of Ireland Act,
1920

—— Limit of historic Ulster province

(after Davies)

opens the new provincial parliament and makes eloquent plea for reconciliation. Within a month, however, over 20 die in Belfast in continuing sectarian violence.

1921

Truce ends war of independence on 11 July. In October, Sinn Fein sends delegates to London to negotiate a treaty between Southern Ireland and Great Britain. A treaty is finally agreed and signed on 6 December, granting dominion status, similar to Canada, to Southern Ireland – to be known as the Irish Free State – but stopping short of the full republican demand. The island remains partitioned, but a Boundary Commission will re-examine the line of partition.

1922

Treaty settlement immediately causes a split in Sinn Fein. Those in favour, principally Arthur Griffith and Michael Collins, argue that it is independence in substance. Opponents, led by de Valera, argue that it betrays republican ideals and retains an oath of allegiance to the British monarch. Dail approves the terms of the treaty by a narrow margin. De Valera resigns. Collins heads an interim administration, while Griffith, restored to leadership of Sinn Fein, continues to lead parallel Dail government.

1922

Widespread violence continues in Northern Ireland. Craig and Collins agree a pact intended to protect northern Catholics in return for the restraining of IRA attacks in Northern Ireland. It has little effect. Sectarian violence reaches an unprecedented crescendo in the summer: widespread atrocity, reprisal and counter-reprisal.

1922

IRA elements opposed to the Treaty form separate command structure and reject the authority of Dail Eireann.

1922

Anti-Treaty irregulars occupy the Four Courts. Collins, under pressure from London, uses artillery to root them out, thus marking the opening of the civil war. The republicans are quickly driven back on their Munster heartland, but even there they have lost control of the cities and towns within two months. The rest of the country is quickly maintained under government control.

1922

Griffith and Collins die within two weeks of each other, Griffith from a cerebral haemorrhage, Collins from a sniper's bullet in an ambush. W.T. Cosgrave the new head of the provisional government.

1922

The constitution of the new Irish Free State is approved by the Dail. The new state formally comes into existence on the first anniversary of the signing of the Anglo-Irish treaty. Policy of executing republican prisoners begins; in all, 77 men will die in this fashion.

1923

Civil war ends in April, with republican order to "dump arms".

1923

James Larkin returns to Ireland after nine years in the United States; splits with his old union, the ITGWU, and forms Workers' Union of Ireland.

From January 1920 the Royal Irish Constabulary was reinforced by the recruitment of British ex-soldiers and sailors, and by November 1921 almost 10,000 of them were in the country. Issued on their arrival with khaki army trousers and dark green police uniforms they quickly became dubbed the Black and Tans. Their reputation for brutality only served to alienate the public more from the RIC.

1923

Censorship of films introduced in the Irish Free State.

1923

Civic Guard renamed Garda Siochana (Guardians of the Peace).

1924

Army Mutiny: army officers oppose proposed demobilisation and severe reduction in army numbers. Situation defused within a week.

1924

Ministers and Secretaries Act regularises the organisation of the higher civil service in the Free State.

1924

Leinster House passed from the Royal Dublin Society to the Irish government.

1925

Boundary Commission established under the terms of the Anglo-Irish treaty fails to agree on significant

1926

Fianna Fail

Percentage of first-preference votes for Fianna Fail, 1932

- 51 or over
- 41 to 50
- 31 to 40
- 30 or under

Distribution of agricultural holdings, by province, 1932

LEINSTER

MUNSTER

CONNACHT

Number of holdings in thousands

Size of holdings in acres

changes to the border between the Free State and Northern Ireland; findings are leaked to the press, causing bitter disappointment in the Free State and the resignation of its representative on the commission, Eoin Mac Neill.

926

The radio station 2RN, forerunner of RTE, first broadcasts.

926

Split in Sinn Fein on policy of abstention from the Dail. De Valera withdraws from the party with his followers and founds new party, Fianna Fail.

927

Fianna Fail win 44 seats in general election, coming within three of government party Cumann na nGaedheal, but refuse to take their seats because of the requirement to swear the oath of allegiance.

927

Assassination of Kevin O'Higgins, Minister for Justice, widely regarded as the most brilliant and ruthless member of the cabinet. In response, government passes new Electoral Act obliging all candidates to undertake to swear the oath of allegiance if elected, failing which undertaking their candidatures will be deemed invalid.

927

De Valera leads Fianna Fail into the Dail, declaring the oath of allegiance to be merely "an empty formula".

1927

Second election sees both Cumann na nGaedheal and Fianna Fail gain at the expense of smaller parties and independents. Cosgrave returned to office.

1927

Establishment of separate Irish currency, although linked at par to sterling.

1929

Censorship of Publications Act introduces literary censorship in the Free State.

1929

Opening of hydro-electric generating station on River Shannon at Ardnacrusha, near Limerick.

1930

Establishment of Irish Hospitals Sweepstakes.

1930

Irish Free State elected to the council of the League of Nations.

1931

First publication of the *Irish Press*, a newspaper established to represent the views of Fianna Fail.

1931

Statute of Westminster gives greatly increased powers and discretion to dominion parliaments.

1932

General elections returns Fianna Fail to power for the first time. De Valera becomes President of the Executive Council (prime minister).

1932

Army Comrades Association founded; better known as the Blueshirts, it develops into a proto-fascist militia along continental lines.

De Valera becomes President of the Executive Council (prime minister) in 1932.

1932

Thirty-first Eucharistic Congress held in Dublin. Over a million people attend a Mass in the Phoenix Park celebrated by the papal legate.

1932

In redemption of an election pledge, government begins to withhold annuity payments due to the British government under the purchase schemes that financed the various Land Acts. It also begins process that abolishes the oath of allegiance.

1932

As a result, an "economic war" develops between Britain and Ireland in which each side placed tariffs on imports from the other. It has a serious effect on the Irish cattle trade.

1932

De Valera elected chairman of the assembly of the League of Nations in Geneva.

1932

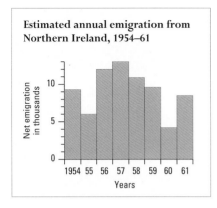

Estimated annual emigration from Northern Ireland, 1954–61

Net emigration in thousands / Years

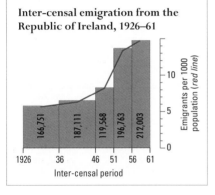

Inter-censal emigration from the Republic of Ireland, 1926–61

Emigrants per 1000 population (*red line*)

166,751 / 187,111 / 119,568 / 196,763 / 212,003

1926 / 36 / 46 / 51 / 56 / 61

Inter-censal period

Few images capture the sense of stasis in the Republic in the 1950s better than those that deal with the chronic emigration of the period, which robbed the state of its most vital resource, its youth, many of whom left with bitterness in their hearts at the failure of their own government to provide for its people. The statistics from the north hide a considerably higher rate of Catholic as opposed to Protestant emigration which helped bolster the latter's rule by keeping the demographic gap intact.

1932
Opening of new parliament building in Northern Ireland, at Stormont in east Belfast.

1932
Protests in Belfast against widespread unemployment caused by the international economic recession unite workers briefly across the sectarian divide.

1933
Eoin O'Duffy dismissed as commissioner of the Garda Siochana; becomes leader of the Blueshirts.

1933
Cumann na nGaedheal unites with the small National Centre Party to form the United Ireland party, later Fine Gael.

1934
Eoin O'Duffy resigns as leader of Fine Gael, which now moves to distance itself from the Blueshirts.

1935
W.T. Cosgrave new leader of Fine Gael, reasserting the primacy of the Cumann na nGaedheal tradition following the O'Duffy interlude.

1935
Shipyard of Workman Clark in Belfast ("the wee yard") closes, a victim of the international economic depression.

1935
Silver jubilee of the

accession of King George V leads to sectarian rioting in Belfast.

1935
Anglo-Irish coal-cattle pact, in which Britain undertakes to increase imports of Irish cattle and Ireland undertakes to buy coal only from Britain – the first sign of an easing in the economic war.

1936
First flight by an Aer Lingus plane, from Dublin to Bristol.

1936
A party of about 700 Blueshirts under Eoin O'Duffy depart for Spain to support Franco's Nationalists in the Spanish Civil War. They saw little or no action during an undistinguished stay. A party of about 200 republicans and socialists under Frank Ryan join the International Brigades in support of the Republic and fight with great distinction and sacrifice.

1936
De Valera's government declares the IRA an illegal organisation.

1937
New constitution replaces that of 1922, renames the Irish Free State as "Eire, or, in the English language, Ireland", but stops short of declaring the state a republic, although a president replaces the governor-general as head of state. It asserts a territorial claim to the entire island. The head of government will henceforth be titled "Taoiseach" (chief or leader, cognate with "führer" and "duce").

1948

938
Anglo-Irish Agreement ends the Economic War. Ireland pays £10 million in final settlement of land annuities issue; Britain returns three ports retained for use of the Royal Navy under the terms of the 1921 treaty; most economic tariffs are removed.

938
Dr Douglas Hyde first President of Ireland.

938
De Valera elected president of the assembly of the League of Nations.

938
Short & Harland aircraft factory opens in Belfast.

939
IRA bombing campaign in Britain. Five killed and 70 injured in explosion in Coventry.

939
Opening of Shannon Airport.

939
Offences Against the State Act introduced by the de Valera government.

939
Second World War. Northern Ireland joins British war effort. South remains neutral; a state of emergency declared for the duration of the war, known officially thereafter as "The Emergency".

939
IRA launch successful raid on the Magazine Fort in the Phoenix Park, Dublin, a major Irish army arms depot. In just over an hour, they remove thirteen lorry loads of ammunition, over a million rounds. This

represented the army's entire reserve supply.

1940
Sean Russell, chief of staff of the IRA, dies aboard a German submarine off the west coast of Ireland.

1941
Heavy German bombing of Belfast results in almost 1,000 deaths and massive destruction of housing and industry.

1942
US troops based in Northern Ireland.

1942
Establishment of Central Bank of Ireland.

1942
IRA murder two RUC constables in Northern Ireland.

1943
Sir Basil Brooke (later Lord Brookeborough) prime minister of Northern Ireland.

1944
Split in Labour Party, as five members of ITGWU secede and form National Labour Party.

1944
Richard Mulcahy succeeds W.T. Cosgrave as leader of Fine Gael.

1944
The so-called "American Note": David Gray, American minister in Dublin, asks de Valera to expel ambassadors of the Axis powers. De Valera refuses.

1945
Split in Irish Trade Union Congress.

1945
At the end of World War II,

de Valera offers his condolences to the German ambassador on the death of Hitler, a controversial expression of neutralist punctilio.

1945
Churchill attacks Eire's neutrality in his victory speech. De Valera's dignified reply regarded as his finest oratorical triumph.

1945
Sean T. O'Kelly second President of Eire in succession to Douglas Hyde.

1946
Eire applies for membership of newly formed United Nations; application vetoed by the Soviet Union.

1947
One of the coldest winters on record, made worse by the continuing post-war austerity measures and shortages. Bread is rationed.

1947
Education Act in Northern Ireland guarantees secondary education for all children with increased state funding.

1947
Shannon the world's first duty-free airport.

1948
Fianna Fail defeated in general election. John A. Costello replaces de Valera as Taoiseach at the head of an inter-party government comprising members of Fine Gael, Labour and Clann na Poblachta.

1948
Establishment of Waterford Glass factory.

1948

1948

The new Taoiseach, John A. Costello, while on a visit to Canada, announces Eire's intention of declaring itself a full republic.

1949

Formal establishment of the Republic of Ireland, which ceases to be a member of the British Commonwealth.

1949

Ireland declines to join newly-established NATO because of Britain's claim of sovereignty in Northern Ireland.

1949

Ireland a founder-member of the Council of Europe.

1949

Ireland accepts jurisdiction of the European Court of Human Rights.

1950

Split in the Labour Party ends. William Norton the leader of the reunited party.

1950

Dublin and Belfast governments agree on plan for the management of the Lough Foyle fisheries.

1950

Establishment of the Industrial Development Authority in the Republic.

1951

Mother and Child Scheme sponsored by the Minister for Health, Noel Browne, meets fierce opposition from Catholic hierarchy and causes church-state crisis which the church wins hands down. Abandoned by his party leader – Sean MacBride – and other cabinet colleagues, Browne resigns.

1951

General election in the republic sees the defeat of the inter-party government and the return of Fianna Fail under de Valera.

1951

Abbey Theatre, Dublin, destroyed by fire.

1951

First Wexford Opera Festival.

1951

Establishment of the Arts Council in the Republic.

1952

Establishment of Bord Iascaigh Mhara (Irish Fisheries Board).

1952

Establishment of the Irish Management Institute.

1952

Adoption Act stipulates that adopters must be of the same religion as the natural parents of the adoptive child or in the case of the adoption of an illegitimate child of the child's mother.

1953

Mother and Child scheme acceptable to the Catholic hierarchy enacted by Fianna Fail government.

1953

Establishment of Gael-Linn to promote Irish language and culture.

1953

Newly crowned Queen Elizabeth II pays first visit to Northern Ireland.

1953

Opening of Chester Beatty Library in Dublin.

1953

Opening of Busaras, the central bus station in Dublin, the first major civic building in the city centre built in a recognisably modern style.

1954

Flags and Emblems Act in Northern Ireland makes it an offence to interfere with the flying of the union flag while giving the RUC power to remove other emblems – specifically the tricolour – that might provoke a breach of the peace.

1954

General election in the Republic sees the defeat of de Valera and the return of Costello at the head of second inter-party government.

1954

IRA attack Gough Barracks, Armagh and commandeer 250 rifles, 37 Sten guns, 9 Bren guns and 40 training rifles. A further raid on Omagh barracks fails.

1955

National Farmers' Association (later IFA) founded.

1955

Republic of Ireland admitted to membership of the United Nations.

1956

Beginning of Operation Harvest, the IRA's border campaign which would splutter on for the next six years. Introduction of internment in Northern Ireland.

1956

T.K. Whitaker appointed secretary of the Department of Finance.

1957

Raid on Brookeborough

police barracks, Co. Fermanagh, by IRA leads to deaths of Sean South and Fergal O'Hanlon, each from the Republic. Emotional scenes at their funerals.

1957

Sean MacBride, the leader of Clann na Poblachta, withdraws support from Costello governement because of Taoiseach's overt hostility to the IRA campaign. Fianna Fail wins subsequent election: de Valera Taoiseach once again.

1957

De Valera's government introduces internment in the Republic.

1957

During the first Dublin Theatre Festival, director Alan Simpson is arrested and charged with mounting an obscene production – Tennessee Williams' *The Rose Tattoo*. The charge is dismissed in court.

1957

Republic joins the International Monetary Fund and the World Bank.

1957

Catholics in Fethard-on-Sea, Co. Wexford, begin boycott of their Protestant neighbours after a dispute over which religion the children of a mixed marriage were to be raised in. De Valera vigorously denounces the boycott.

1958

First Aer Lingus transatlantic service.

1958

Republic repeals legislation dating from the 1930s which restricted foreign ownership of

manufacturing industry in the state.

1958

Publication of first Programme for Economic Expansion, a seminal moment in the recovery of Irish economy and society.

1959

De Valera finally retires from active politics. Sean Lemass succeeds as Taoiseach. De Valera succeeds Sean T. O'Kelly as President.

1959

End of split in Irish trade union movement with formation of the Irish Congress of Trade Unions.

1959

Republic votes in a constitutional referendum to retain proportional representation by the single-transferable vote as the voting system despite government attempts to introduce British first-past-the-post system.

1959

First broadcast by Ulster Television.

1960

F.H. Boland elected president of the General Assembly of the UN.

1960

Nine Irish troops serving with UN peace keeping force in the Congo killed in an ambush at Niemba.

1961

First broadcast by Telefis Eireann (later RTE television).

1961

Census shows record low population in the Republic. Population has declined steadily since independence.

1961

Republic applies for membership of European Economic Community (now EU).

1961

Republic joins UNESCO.

1961

Lemass continues as Taoiseach after general election as head of a minority Fianna Fail government.

During his 1963 visit, President John F. Kennedy received his patent of arms prepared by the Chief Herald of Ireland.

1962

End of IRA's border campaign.

1962

First edition of "Late, Late Show" on Telefis Eireann; it would go on to be the longest-running chat show in the world.

1963

Visit of President John F. Kennedy to Ireland, four months before his assassination.

1963

1963
Captain Terence O'Neill succeeds Lord Brookeborough as leader of the Unionist Party and prime minister of Northern Ireland.

1963
Rev. Ian Paisley leads protests of Protestant ultras against tributes paid on the death of Pope John XXIII.

1964
Campaign for Social Justice established in Dungannon, Co. Tyrone. It was the remote ancestor of the civil rights movement in the province.

1964
Fine Gael adopts "Just Society" programme proposed by Declan Costello, moving the party to the left of its previously very conservative positions on social and economic issues.

1964
Rioting in Belfast as police remove tricolour from the headquarters of a republican candidate in Belfast under the powers granted by the Flags and Emblems Act.

1965
Sean Lemass and Terence O'Neill meet at Stormont and later in Dublin in an attempt to improve the traditionally frosty relations between the two parts of the island.

1965
Nationalist Party in Northern Ireland agrees to assume the role of official opposition.

1965
Lockwood Committee on the future of higher education in Northern Ireland recommends Coleraine as site of new university, not Derry as had been expected. Widely regarded as a sectarian decision, it overshadowed other recommendations in the report.

1965
Investment in Education published in the republic. It contains the blueprint for a revolution in Irish education.

1965
Liam Cosgrave, son of W.T. Cosgrave, new leader of Fine Gael.

1965
Anglo-Irish Free Trade Area Agreement provides for progressive removal of protective tariffs in Anglo-Irish trade.

1966
Destruction of Nelson Pillar, Dublin, by IRA bomb.

1966
Golden Jubilee of 1916 Rising: official celebrations in the Republic; sectarian violence in Northern Ireland.

1966
Opening of new Abbey Theatre in Dublin.

1966
Donogh O'Malley, Minister for Education, announces the forthcoming introduction of free secondary education in the Republic.

1966
Widespread protests by National Farmers' Association culminate in mass march on Dublin and sit-down outside the Department of Agriculture.

1966
Lemass resigns as Taoiseach; succeeded by Jack Lynch.

1967
Inaugural meeting of Northern Ireland Civil Rights Association in Belfast.

1967
Legislation in the Republic liberalises the literary censorship and removes its traditional ferocity.

1968
Papal encyclical *Humanae Vitae*, reiterates traditional Catholic ban on contraception and begins first significant public debate among Irish Catholics on a matter of church teaching.

1968
The New University of Ulster opens at Coleraine, Co. Derry.

1968
Major clashes in Derry between members of the Northern Ireland Civil Rights Association (NICRA) and the RUC. The march had gone ahead despite a government ban. Pictures of police brutality against unarmed marchers are flashed around the world.

1968
Radicalisation of Catholic/nationalist opinion in Northern Ireland, especially among the young, leads to an increase in street demonstrations and brings counter-demonstrations from loyalists.

1969

1968

In response, O'Neill's government announces reform package to remove some of the more egregious forms of discrimination.

1968

O'Neill sacks William Craig, his hard-line Minister of Home Affairs.

1969

March by People's Democracy, a mainly student radical group, from Belfast to Derry, is ambushed at Burntollet Bridge, by armed loyalist mob abetted by RUC and B Specials. A key moment in the descent of Northern Ireland into civil chaos.

1969

Brian Faulkner, Minister of Commerce, resigns from O'Neill's cabinet.

1969

Northern Ireland general election shows Unionists to be divided 2:1 in favour of O'Neill. However, this proves a Pyrrhic victory and he resigns some weeks later. Succeeded by Major James Chichester-Clark, who defeats the ambitious and talented Faulkner by a single vote.

1969

Jack Lynch wins overall majority for Fianna Fail in Republic's general election.

1969

Complete collapse of civil order throughout many parts of Northern Ireland. Battle of the Bogside in Derry creates a no-go area for the forces of the state, while horrific burnings of houses and other premises take place in Belfast. British army deployed to take over peace-keeping duties.

1969

Hunt Report recommends reform of the RUC and abolition of the B Specials. It is replaced by the Ulster Defence Regiment (UDR), under direct army control.

The summer of 1969 brought the wholesale collapse of civil order in Northern Ireland. In effect, the nationalist-Catholic population withdrew such tacit consent as it had previously granted to the Stormont administration.

TROUBLES

The Irish Free State survived the deaths of its two leading founders, Arthur Griffith and Michael Collins, during the civil war, and established its legitimacy. In 1932, Eamon de Valera, political leader of the anti-Treaty side, won a general election and took control of the country in a remarkably peaceful transfer of power. His party, Fianna Fail, has dominated southern politics ever since. For a generation, Fianna Fail conducted an ultimately disastrous experiment in protectionist economics; only with a switch to a free trade regime in the 1960s did the economy begin to take advantage of the long economic boom in the western world that followed World War II. In the meantime, the Free State had unstitched some of the more controversial aspects of the 1921 treaty, declared itself a republic and left the British Commonwealth.

These more assertive manifestations of nationalist sensibility did nothing to improve relations between the Republic and Northern Ireland, which remained extremely chilly. The fact that the Republic had remained neutral during World War II while Northern Ireland – as part of the UK – was a combatant had not helped. Northern Ireland quickly developed a Protestant laagar mentality: the state existed specifically for the convenience of its Protestant majority and it quickly institutionalised sectarian practices. Local elections were gerrymandered to produce Unionist majorities even where there was a local Catholic (i.e. nationalist) majority. The police and the police reserve were overwhelmingly Protestant: harassment of Catholics was commonplace. Local authority housing was allocated on a sectarian basis, not on grounds of need.

Protestants in Northern Ireland lived in a state of constant low-level hysteria, obsessed by the Catholic fifth column within. The Catholic population was never less than 35 per cent of the whole and there were local Catholic majorities in many areas of the province, especially in the west. In fairness, Protestant fears were not entirely groundless. The IRA had done all in its power back in 1920–22 to prevent the birth of Northern Ireland: there was horrifying

violence, especially in the Belfast area, over three successive summers. But whatever the IRA could inflict, the
forces of the state – often behaving no better than licensed
mobs – could inflict worse, and did. The net effect of the
bloody birth of Northern Ireland was to confirm Catholics
in their hatred and resentment of the sectarian state in
which they were trapped and Protestants in their hysterical
suspicion of all nationalists.

The stand-off lasted until the 1960s. There was a gener-
ational change in political leadership north and south.
Cross-border talks on matters of mutual co-operation
began and there were other signs of a thaw. A hopelessly
inept IRA campaign from 1956 to 1962 had failed and
seemed to mark the last gasp of violent republicanism. The
nationalist demand switched to incremental rather than
constitutional issues. Picking up the contemporary theme
from the United States, the call was now for civil rights:
equal rights as UK citizens.

These demands – an end to multiple voting and electoral gerrymandering, fair housing allocation according to
genuine need, repeal of the ferociously illiberal Special
Powers Act and the disbandment of the sectarian police
reserve – would have been unexceptional in a normal society. In Northern Ireland, they mobilised the forces of the
state. Civil rights marchers were batoned off the streets by
the police. Loyalist counter-demonstrations, often led by
the emerging figure of Rev. Ian Paisley – a fundamentalist
Protestant with a preacher-man's gift for mob oratory –
underscored the hostility of working-class Protestants to
what they regarded as an IRA plot.

By the summer of 1969, the province had collapsed into
wholesale civil violence and destruction. It was, in a sense,
a renewal of the violence of 1920–22. This time, however,
the world was watching on television. Horrified at what
was happening in this hitherto hidden corner of the United
Kingdom, the London government sent in troops to keep
the two sides apart when it was clear that the police had
totally lost control of the situation. It proved easier to get
them in than to get them out again.

When the violence of 1968–69 broke out, the IRA were
nowhere to be seen. Since the end of the border campaign
in 1962, the movement had been led by a southern leadership looking for new directions and hoping to find it in the
modish socialism of the 1960s. So republican energies were
focused on radical social issues of all sorts, which was less
than useless to beleaguered Belfast Catholic ghettos in the
summer of 1969. The IRA's most basic role was to defend

*Inter-communal violence has a
long and depressing history in
Northern Ireland. This
newspaper headline dates
from 1935, at which time the
tradition of civil unrest was
already almost a century old.*

its own vulnerable communities from sectarian attack.

The republican movement split as a result of these pressures. The southern leadership assumed the titles "Official Sinn Fein/IRA", while a mainly northern breakaway group, more concerned with urgent communal defence than with socialist ideology, formed the Provisional republican movement. The Provisional IRA were to be the key motor of the Troubles to come.

The British army's honeymoon period lasted barely six months. The Provos went from communal defence to an aggressive guerrilla war aimed at forcing a British withdrawal from Northern Ireland. Loyalist paramilitaries formed a menacing sectarian counterpoise on the Protestant side. The devolved Northern Ireland parliament was prorogued in 1972 and London took over direct control of the province. An attempt at cross-community compromise was scuppered by loyalist intransigence in 1974. Northern Ireland settled into a low-level, squalid and morally debilitating conflict, in which no group – British army, Provos or loyalists – were strong

Margaret Thatcher and Garret FitzGerald, whose governments negotiated the Anglo-Irish Agreement of 1985 which gave Dublin an input into the affairs of Northern Ireland, much to the fury of unionists.

enough to force a victory. The Provos underwent a long conversion from military to political action, but not before they had been responsible for almost 2,000 of the 3,000 deaths in the Troubles. The Belfast Agreement of 1998 represented a wobbly compromise between the various parties, but there remains a fundamental absence of cross-community trust. The basis for a normal civil society does not exist in Northern Ireland.

Since the 1960s, policy in the Republic has concentrated on the country's position in the European Union. A brief economic boom was followed by the wasted years from the mid 70s to the mid 80s, then a period of slow recovery and finally the spectacular, if uneven, boom of the late 1990s. The priorities of the Republic remain economic, those of Northern Ireland constitutional.

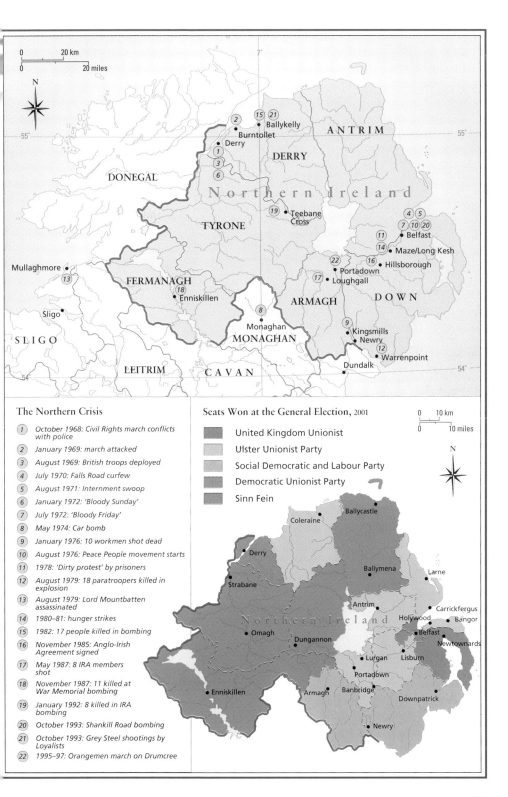

The Northern Crisis

1. October 1968: Civil Rights march conflicts with police
2. January 1969: march attacked
3. August 1969: British troops deployed
4. July 1970: Falls Road curfew
5. August 1971: Internment swoop
6. January 1972: 'Bloody Sunday'
7. July 1972: 'Bloody Friday'
8. May 1974: Car bomb
9. January 1976: 10 workmen shot dead
10. August 1976: Peace People movement starts
11. 1978: 'Dirty protest' by prisoners
12. August 1979: 18 paratroopers killed in explosion
13. August 1979: Lord Mountbatten assassinated
14. 1980–81: hunger strikes
15. 1982: 17 people killed in bombing
16. November 1985: Anglo-Irish Agreement signed
17. May 1987: 8 IRA members shot
18. November 1987: 11 killed at War Memorial bombing
19. January 1992: 8 killed in IRA bombing
20. October 1993: Shankill Road bombing
21. October 1993: Grey Steel shootings by Loyalists
22. 1995–97: Orangemen march on Drumcree

Seats Won at the General Election, 2001

- United Kingdom Unionist
- Ulster Unionist Party
- Social Democratic and Labour Party
- Democratic Unionist Party
- Sinn Fein

1970

1970

Sinn Fein and IRA split into Official and Provisional wings, corresponding to those who favour left-wing, socialist agitation and those who favour a more traditional and urgent response to the civil disturbances in Northern Ireland.

1970

Rev. Ian Paisley first elected to Stormont in Terence O'Neill's former constituency.

Lynch on suspicion of involvement in a conspiracy to import arms illegally for distribution to the IRA in the north. A third minister, Kevin Boland, resigns in sympathy. Charges are later preferred against the two sacked ministers and others but all are acquitted.

1970

Foundation of the Social Democratic and Labour Party (SDLP) which supplants the Nationalist Party as the chief political voice of the anti-unionist community.

attempted loyalist incursion into the Short Strand, an isolated Catholic salient in east Belfast, was stopped not by the British army but by members of the Provisional IRA, who held the steeple of St Matthew's church and killed four loyalists.

1970

An army-imposed curfew on the Lower Falls marks the final breach between the British army and the Catholic working-class. Recruitment for the Provisional IRA soars.

1971

Continuing deterioration of situation in Northern Ireland.

1971

Chichester-Clark resigns, succeeded as prime minister of Northern Ireland by Brian Faulkner.

1971

SDLP withdraws from Stormont.

1971

Introduction of internment without trial by Faulkner government in Northern Ireland. A disastrous misjudgement, its folly was compounded by incompetence as security information on which suspects were apprehended was out of date. Huge upsurge in nationalist discontent.

1971

Founding of the Democratic Unionist Party (DUP) under leadership of Ian Paisley.

1972

The most destructive year in the history of the Northern Ireland troubles:

Jack Lynch (Taoiseach 1966–73, 1977–79) signing the treaty of accession to the European Economic Community on behalf of the Republic of Ireland in 1973.

1970

Formation of non-sectarian Alliance Party of Northern Ireland in an attempt to represent middle ground.

1970

Arms crisis in the Republic. Two cabinet ministers – Charles Haughey and Neil Blaney – are sacked by Jack

1970

Inter-communal hatred and riots lead to increased deployment of troops and inevitable clashes between nationalist rioters and the army. Progressive deterioration of relations throughout the year as Provisional IRA begins to flex its muscles. An

470 deaths; over 10,000 shootings; almost 2,000 bombs planted; 531 people charged with terrorist offences.

1973
Ireland and the UK join the European Economic Community (now the European Union).

1973
Sunningdale Agreement sets up devolved power-sharing executive in Northern Ireland.

1974
Power-sharing executive under chief executive Brian Faulkner (pro-agreement Unionist) and deputy chief executive Gerry Fitt (SDLP) collapses in face of general strike by anti-agreement Ulster Workers' Council. Direct rule re-imposed.

1979
Pope John Paul II visits Ireland, the only papal visit to date.

1979
Republic of Ireland enters the European Monetary System, thus breaking the link with sterling.

1979
Charles Haughey leader of Fianna Fail and Taoiseach. Margaret Thatcher prime minister of the UK.

1981
Ten republicans die in hunger strikes in Northern Ireland prisons in pursuit of special category status.

1985
Anglo-Irish Agreement signed by Taoiseach Garret FitzGerald and Margaret Thatcher at Hillsborough Castle, Co. Down: established a joint

secretariat to monitor and consult on government in Northern Ireland. Vociferous but futile protests from unionists.

1987
Remembrance Sunday bomb in Enniskillen, Co. Fermanagh, one of the worst atrocities of the troubles, kills eleven and injures many more.

1989
Charles Haughey forms first ever Fianna Fail-led coalition government in the Republic in alliance with the Progressive Democrats under Desmond O'Malley.

1992
Bishop Eamonn Casey of Galway forced to emigrate after discovery that he was the father of a teenage son; the first of a succession of sexual scandals – many of them distressing cases of child sexual abuse involving episcopal prevarication and neglect – that compromised the moral authority of the Irish Catholic church.

1993
Downing Street declaration by Prime Minister John Major and Taoiseach Albert Reynolds.

1994
IRA ceasefire.

1995
Beginning of unprecedented economic boom in the Republic – the Celtic Tiger – that lasts until 2001.

1996
End of IRA ceasefire.

1998
Good Friday Agreement brings a hoped-for end of

the troubles and restores a devolved power-sharing executive to Northern Ireland.

2002
Republic adopts the euro, while Northern Ireland – as part of the UK – retains sterling.

2002
Disagreement over pace of decommissioning of paramilitary weapons leads to suspension of Northern Ireland executive and resumption of direct rule.

Mary Robinson's success in the 1990 presidential elections broke the mould. A champion of women's rights, a left-of-centre social progressive, her victory shook the conservative, male-dominated hold on Irish politics.

Further Reading

Aalen, F. H. A., Kevin Whelan & Matthew Stout (eds), *Atlas of the Irish Rural Landscape,* Cork University Press, 1997.

Bardon, Jonathan, *A History of Ulster,* Blackstaff, 1992.

Barnard, T. C., *Cromwellian Ireland: English Government and Reform in Ireland, 1649–60,* Clarendon Press, 1975.

Brown, Terence, *Ireland: a Social and Cultural History, 1922–79,* Fontana, 1981.

Canny, Nicholas P., *The Elizabethan Conquest of Ireland: A Pattern Established, 1565–76,* Harvester Press, 1976.

de Paor, Máire and Liam, *Early Christian Ireland,* Thames & Hudson, 1978.

Duffy, Seán, *Ireland in the Middle Ages,* Gill & Macmillan, 1997.

Duffy, Seán, et al. *Atlas of Irish History,* Gill & Macmillan, 1997.

Duffy, Seán, *Concise History of Ireland,* Gill & Macmillan, 2000.

Ellis, Steven G., *Tudor Ireland: Crown, Community and the Conflict of Cultures, 1470–1603,* Longman, 1985.

Foster, R. F. , *Modern Ireland, 1600–1972,* Penguin, 1988. (ed) *The Oxford Illustrated History of Ireland,* Oxford University Press, 1989.

Gillespie, Raymond, *Colonial Ulster: The Settlement of East Ulster, 1600–1641,* Cork University Press, 1985.

Harbison, Peter, *Pre-Christian Ireland,* Thames & Hudson, 1988. (ed) *The Shell Guide to Ireland,* Gill & Macmillan, 1989.

Kelly, James, *Prelude to Union: Anglo-Irish Politics in the 1780s*, Cork University Press, 1992.

Kinealy, Christine, *This Great Calamity, The Irish Famine, 1845-52*, Gill & Macmillan, 1994.

Lee, Joseph, *Ireland, 1912–85*, Cambridge University Press, 1989.

Lennon, Colm, *Sixteenth-Century Ireland*, Gill & Macmillan, 1994.

Lydon, James, *The Lordship of Ireland in the Middle Ages*, Gill & Macmillan, 1972.

Lyons, F. S. L. (ed), *Ireland since the Famine*, Fontana, 1973.

Meehan, Bernard, *The Book of Kells*, Thames & Hudson, 1994.

Mitchell, Frank, *The Shell Guide to Reading the Irish Landscape*, Country House, 1986.

Ó Corráin, Donncha, *Ireland before the Normans*, Gill & Macmillan, 1972.

O'Kelly, M. J., *Early Ireland*, Cambridge University Press, 1989.

O'Ríordáin, S. P., *Antiquities of the Irish Countryside*, Methuen, 1979.

Otway-Ruthven, A. J., *A History of Medieval Ireland*, Ernest Benn, 1968, 1980.

Stalley, Roger, *The Cistercian Monasteries of Ireland*, Yale University Press, 1987.

INDEX

Abbey Theatre 82, 96, 98
Act of Union 68
Adomnan, St 13
Aer Lingus 94, 97
Affane, battle of 37
Aidan, St 13, 17
Alliance Party 104
American Note, the 95
Anglo-Irish Free Trade
  Agreement 98
Annaghdown 69
Annals of Innisfallen 19
Annals of the Four Masters
  44
Anne, Queen 60
Anti-Partition League 88
Ardnacrusha 93
Armagh 19, 20
Armagh, Book of 19
Arms crisis 104
Army Comrades Association,
  see Blueshirts
Army Mutiny 91
Ascendancy, Protestant 52,
  62–63
Ashe, Thomas 88
Asquith, H.H. 82
Athenry 24
Athlone 59
Aughrim, battle of 59
Augustine, St 13
Auxiliaries 89
B Specials 99
Back Lane Parliament, *see*
  Catholic convention
Bagenal, Henry 41
Balbriggan 89
Ballingarry 74
Ballynahinch, battle of 68
Ballyshannon 31, 41
Baltimore, Co. Cork 44
Bangor 13
Bank of Ireland 66
Bann, River 34
Bantry Bay 68
Barrow, River 9, 28
Battle of the Diamond 66
Belach Lechta, battle of 19
Belfast *News-Letter* 60
Belfast 44, 75, 76, 89, 94, 95,
  98–105

Benburb, battle of 47
Beresford, John 63
Bingham, Richard 39, 41
Black and Tans 89
Black Death 30
Blaney, Neil 104
Bloody Sunday (1920) 89
Blount, Charles, Lord
  Mountjoy 42–43
Blueshirts, 93–94
Boland, F.H. 97
Boland, Kevin 104
Boleyn, Anne 35
Book of Common Prayer 37
Boundary Commission
  91–92
Boycott, Charles 78
Boyle, Richard, 1st earl of
  Cork 44, 50
Boyne Valley 9–10, 19
Boyne, battle of 10, 59
Boyne, River 9
Brian Boru 19, 26
Brigid, St 13, 24
Broighter Hoard 12
Bronze Age 12
Brooke, Basil 95, 98
Brookeborough, Lord, *see*
  Brooke, Basil
Browne, Noel 96
Bruce, Edward 28
Buckingham Palace
  Conference 86
Bunratty Castle 24
Burke, Edmund 62
Burke, Thomas 79
Burke/de Burgo family 24, 37
Butler, "Black Tom", *see*
  Butler, Thomas, 10th earl
  of Ormond
Butler, James, 12th earl/1st
  duke of Ormond 45–48,
  56–57
Butler, Thomas, 10th earl of
  Ormond 39
Butt, Isaac 76
Callan 31
Canterbury 19
Carrickfergus 23, 25, 30, 47,
  59, 64
Carson, Edward 82

Casement, Roger 86
Casey, Eamonn 105
Cashel 19, 20
Castlecomer 44
Castledermot 28
Cathach 13
Catherine of Aragon 35
Catholic Association 69
Catholic Committee 64
Catholic convention 66
Catholic Defence Association
  75
Catholic Emancipation 69
Catholic Relief Acts 63, 66
Catholic Truth Society of
  Ireland 81
Catholic University 75, 79
Cavendish, Lord Frederick 79
Ceide Fields 8
Celtic Tiger 105
Celts 10, 26
Censorship 91, 93, 98
Charles I, King 44–48
Charles II, King 55, 57
Chester Beatty Library 96
Chichester, Arthur 43
Chichester-Clark, James 99
Christ Church cathedral,
  Dublin 19, 59
Christian Brothers 68
Christianity 16, 26
Church of Ireland 37, 45, 56,
  64, 76
Churchill, Lord Randolph 80
Ciaran, St 13
Cistercians 24, 30, 34
Civil War 91
Clan na Gael 78
Clann na Poblachta 95, 97
Clare by-elections (1828–29)
  69
Clarke, Thomas J. 79, 88
Clifford, Conyers 42
Clonmacnoise 13, 19
Clontarf, battle of 19
Clontibret, battle of 41
Coleraine 44, 98
Colleen Bawn, *see* Hanley,
  Ellen
Collins Barracks 68–69
Collins, Michael 89–91, 100

Colum Cille, St 13, 17
Columbanus, St 13, 17
Comgall, St 13
Composition of Connacht
    39
Comyn, John 23
Confederation of Kilkenny
    46–48
Connolly, James 81, 86, 88
Conolly, William 60
Contraception 98
Cooke, Henry 69
Coote, Charles 46
Cork Examiner 72
Cosgrave, Liam 98
Cosgrave, W.T. 91, 93, 94, 95
Costello, Declan 98
Costello, John A. 95, 96
Council of Europe 96
Craig, James 89, 91
Craig, William 99
Cromwell, Henry 54
Cromwell, Oliver 48–55
Cromwell, Richard 55
Cullen, Paul 75, 76, 78
Cumann na nGaedheal 93,
    94
Curlew Mountains, battle of
    42
Curragh Mutiny 86
Custom House, Dublin 66
Dail Eireann 85, 89, 91
Dal Cais, kingdom of 19
Dalriada, kingdom of 13
Davies, John, 43
Davitt, Michael 76, 78
de Courcy, John 23, 24
de Lacy, Hugh 23, 24,27
de Marisco, Geoffrey 24
de Midia, Petronilla 30
De Valera, Eamon 88–90,
    93–97, 100
Deasy's Act 76
Declaratory Act 60, 66
del Aguila, Don Juan 43
Democratic Unionist Party
    104
Deputy's Pass, battle of
    41–42
Derry 13, 43, 44, 89, 98–99
Derry, siege of 59

Desmond rebellions 39
Desmond, earldom of 28, 30,
    31, 34, 39
Disraeli, Benjamin 76
Dolly's Brae 74
Dominicans 24
Donnelly, Dan 68
Donnybrook Fair 75
Dowcra, Sir Henry 42–43
Down Survey 54–55
Downpatrick 30
Dowth 8, 9
Drogheda 9, 32, 48, 52
Druim Cett, convention of
    13
Dublin Bay 9
Dublin Castle 63
Dublin Metropolitan Police
    (DMP) 72
Dublin, city 9, 19, 20, 23, 26,
    27, 33
Dublin, county 24
Dún an Óir 39
Dundalk 28
Dungannon 44
Durrow, Book of 13
Dysert O'Dea, battle of 28
Easter Rising 85, 86, 98
Economic war 93–95
Edward III, King 30
Edward IV, King 31, 32
Edward VI, King 37
Edward VII, King, 82
Elizabeth I, Queen 39, 43, 50
Elizabeth II, Queen 96
Emain Macha 12, 13
Emmet, Robert 68
Enniscorthy 68
Enniskillen 41, 105
Erne, River 31
Essex, earl of 41
Eucharistic Congress 93
Euro (currency) 105
European Court of Human
    Rights, 96
European Economic
    Community, *see* European
    Union
European Union (EU) 97,
    102, 105
Famine (1740–41) 60, 64

Famine (1845–52), *see* Great
    Famine
Faughart, battle of 28
Faulkner, Brian 104–05
Fenians/IRB 75, 76, 84, 86
Fethard-on-Sea 97
Fianna Fail 93–105 *passim*
Fine Gael 94, 95, 98
First World War, *see* Great
    War
Fitt, Gerry 105
Fitton, Alexander 57
fitz Gilbert, Richard, *see*
    Strongbow
fitz William, Raymond le Gros
    23
FitzGerald, Garret 102, 105
FitzGerald, Gearóid Mór, 8th
    earl of Kildare 32
FitzGerald, Gearóid Óg, 9th
    earl of Kildare 33
FitzGerald, Gerald, 3rd earl of
    Desmond 31
FitzGerald, James Fitzmaurice
    39
FitzGerald, John fitz Thomas
    28
FitzGerald, Thomas, 10th earl
    of Kildare 33, 35, 37
Fitzgibbon, John, Lord Clare
    62–63
Fitzwilliam, 2nd earl 66
Flight of the Earls 43
Flood, Henry 65
Four Courts, Dublin 68, 91
Franklin, Benjamin 64
Freeman's Journal 64
French Revolution 66
Fursa, St 13, 17
Gaelic Athletic Association 79
Gaelic League 81, 86
Gael-Linn 96
Galway 24, 31
Garda Siochana 91, 94
General Post Office, Dublin
    69, 86
George III, King 64, 68
George IV, King 68–69, 72
George V, King 82, 89–90, 94
Georgian architecture 63, 65,
    67

Gearóid Iarla, *see* FitzGerald, Gerald, 3rd Earl
German Plot   88
Gladstone, William Ewart   76–81, 84
Glen Mama, battle of   19
Glorious Revolution   57
Gnaeus Julius Agricola   12
Goldsmith, Oliver   62
Good Friday Agreement   105
Government of Ireland Act   89
Graces, the   44
Grand Canal   64, 66
Grattan, Henry   62
Grattan's parliament, *see* Legislative independence
Gray, David   95
Great Famine   72–75, 84
Great War   86, 89
Grey de Wilton, Lord   39
Grey, Lord Leonard   37
Griffith, Arthur   82, 88, 90, 91, 100
Guinness, Arthur   64
Ha'penny Bridge, Dublin   68–69
Handel, Georg Friedrich   64
Hanley, Ellen   69
Harland & Wolff   76, 82
Haughey, Charles   104–05
Henry II, King   23, 27
Henry III, King   24
Henry IV, King   31
Henry VI, King   32
Henry VII, King   32
Henry VIII, King   32–37, 50
Holycross Abbey   31
Home Rule Bills   80, 81, 83, 86
Home rule   76–81
Howth gun-running   86
Hyde, Douglas   80–81, 83, 95
Ice Age, end of   8
Industrial Development Authority   96
International Monetary Fund (IMF)   97
Internment   104
Invincibles   79
Ireton, Henry   54

Irish Agricultural Organisation Society   81
Irish Citizen Army   86
Irish Confederation   74
Irish Congress of Trade Unions (ICTU)   97
Irish Crown Jewels   82
Irish Free State   85, 91, 100
Irish Hospitals Sweepstakes   93
Irish Loyal and Patriotic Union   79
Irish National Land League, *see* Land League
Irish Press   93
Irish Republican Army (IRA)   85, 89–91, 95, 96–97, 98, 100–105
Irish Republican Brotherhood, *see* Fenians/IRB
Irish Times   75
Irish Trade Union Congress (ITUC)   95
Irish Transport and General Workers' Union (ITGWU)   82, 86, 91, 95
Irish Volunteers   86, 89
Iron Age   12
James I, King,   43, 44, 52
James II, King   57–59
Jesuits, *see* Society of Jesus
John Paul II, Pope   105
John, Prince and King   23, 24, 27, 34
Jones, Michael   47–48
Joy, Francis   60
Julius Caesar   12
Keating, Geoffrey   44
Kennedy, John F.   97
Kildare   24
Kildare, earldom of   28, 34–35, 37
Kilkenny   24, 28
Kilkenny, Statute of   30
Killian, St   13
Killybegs   41
Kilmainham Treaty   79
Kilmichael   89
Kinsale   59
Kinsale, battle of   42–43
Knock, Co. Mayo   78

Knowth   8, 9
Kyteler, Dame Alice   30
Labour Party   95–96
Lake, Gerard   68
Land Acts (1870–1903)   76, 78–79, 82
Land League   78
Larkin, James   82, 91
Larne   28, 86
League of Nations   93, 95
Legislative independence   66
Leighlinbridge   28
Leinster House, Dublin   64, 91
Lemass, Sean   97, 98
Liffey, River   9
Limerick   19, 23
Limerick, sieges of   59
Limerick, treaty of   59
Lindisfarne   13, 17
Lionel of Clarence   30
Lockout (Dublin)   86
Londonderry, *see* Derry
Loughrea   24
Luby, Thomas Clarke   76
Lusitania   86
Lynch, Jack   98
Mac Murrough, Art   31
MacBride, Sean   96, 97
MacCurtain, Thomas   89
MacDonnell, Antony   82
MacMurrough, Dermot/ Diarmaid   21, 23, 26
MacSwiney, Thomas   89
Mael Seachnaill   19
Maguire, Hugh   41
Major, John   105
Malachy, St   20
Manchester Martyrs   76
Marsh's Library, Dublin   59
Marshall, Anselm   24
Marshall, Walter   24
Marshall, William   24
Martyn, Edward   81
Mary, Queen   37
Mathew, Theobald   72
Maynooth   37
McManus, Terence Bellew   76
Meagher, Thomas Francis   74
Mellifont, treaty of   43

Mitchel, John   74
Monasterboice   19
Monasteries   26
Monster meetings   72
Montgomery, Henry   69
Mother and Child Scheme   96
Mount Sandel   8
Mountjoy, Lord, see Blount,
    Charles
Moyry Pass, battle of   43
Mulcahy, Richard   95
Munro, Robert   46–47
Murray, Daniel   75
Nation, The   72
National Gallery of Ireland
    76
National Library of Ireland
    80
National Museum of Ireland
    80
National University of Ireland
    82
National Volunteers   86
Navan fort, see Emain Macha
Navan, 9
Nelson Pillar, Dublin   68, 98
Nendrum   21
New Departure   78
New University of Ulster   98
Newgrange   8, 9–11, 19
Newman, John Henry   75
Ní Chonaill, Eibhlín Dubh
    65
Niemba ambush   97
Nine Years' War   41–43, 50
Nore, River   9
No-rent manifesto   79
Normans   21, 26–27
North Atlantic Treaty
    Organisation (NATO)   96
Northern Ireland Civil Rights
    Association   98
Northern Ireland   89, 91, 95,
    96, 98–105
Norton, William   96
Ó Laoghaire, Art   64
O'Brien, Murrough, Lord
    Inchiquin   46, 48, 54
O'Brien, William Smith   74
O'Brien, William   81
O'Brien's Bridge   32

O'Byrne, Fiach MacHugh   39
O'Byrne, Phelim MacFeagh
    41–42
O'Carolan, Turlough   60
O'Connell, Daniel   69–74
O'Connor, Aed   28
O'Connor, Rory   21, 23, 27
O'Donnell, Hugh (Red Hugh)
    41, 43
O'Donnell, Niall Garbh   31,
    43
O'Donovan Rossa, Jeremiah
    76, 86
O'Duffy, Eoin   94
O'Hanlon, Fergal   97
O'Higgins, Kevin   93
O'Kelly, Sean T.   95, 97
O'Leary, John   76
O'Malley, Desmond   105
O'Malley, Donogh   98
O'More, Owney   41, 43
O'More, Rory   45
O'Neill, Brian   28
O'Neill, Conn Bacach   37
O'Neill, Hugh, earl of Tyrone
    39, 41–44
O'Neill, Matthew   37
O'Neill, Owen Roe   47, 48
O'Neill, Phelim   48, 54
O'Neill, Shane   37, 39
O'Neill, Terence   98–99
O'Neill, Turlough Luineach
    39, 41
O'Reilly, Edmund   55
O'Rourke, Brian Óg   42
O'Shea, Katharine   80
O'Shea, William   80
O'Toole, Lorcan   20
Oates, Titus   57
Offaly, Lord, see FitzGerald,
    Thomas, 10th earl
Ogham   12
Old Pretender, the   64
Ormond, earldom of   30, 31,
    34
Paisley, Ian   98, 101, 104
Pale, the   31
Palladius   12
Parliament House, Dublin
    60, 63
Parliament   28, 31, 32, 37, 56

Parnell, Charles Stewart
    76–80, 84
Pass of the Plumes, battle of
    41
Patrick, St   12, 13, 16
Patriot parliament   59
Pearse, Patrick   82, 84, 86, 88
Pearse, Willie   88
Peel, Robert   68, 72
Penal Laws   59–60
People's Democracy   99
Perrot, Sir John   39
Petty, William   54
Philip II, King of Spain   41
Phoenix Park Murders   79, 80
Pigott, Richard   80
Piltown, battle of   31
Pirates   44
Pitt, William   68
Plan of Campaign   80
Plantation of Ulster   43–44,
    50, 52
Plantation, Cromwellian   54
Plantations, Tudor   37, 50
Plunkett, Horace   81
Plunkett, James Noble, Count
    88
Plunkett, Oliver   56–57
Poor Law   72, 75
Pope's Brass Band, see
    Catholic Defence
    Association
Popish Plot   57
Poulnabrone Dolmen   8
Poynings, Edward   32, 66
Presbyterians   63, 69, 72
Prince regent, see George IV
Proclamation of the Republic
    86
Programme for Economic
    Expansion   97
Progressive Democrats   105
Proleek Dolmen   8
Ptolemy   12
Quarantotti letter   68
Queen's Colleges   72
Radio Telefís Éireann (RTE)
    93, 97
Railways   72
Raleigh, Walter   39
Rebellion of 1641   45, 52

Redmond, John   81, 82–88
Reformation, the   35
Regium donum   56
Renaissance, the,   34–35
Repeal   72
Republic of Ireland   96
Reynolds, Albert   105
Rice, Edmund Ignatius   68
Richard I, King   23, 24
Richard II, King   31, 34
Rinuccini, Giovanni Batista   47–48
Rising of 1798   68
Robinson, Mary   105
Roman Empire   16
Rosse, 3rd earl   72
Rotunda hospital   64
Royal Barracks, see Collins Barracks
Royal Dublin Society   60, 91
Royal Hospital, Dublin   57
Royal Irish Constabulary (RIC)   72, 85, 89
Royal Ulster Constabulary (RUC)   95, 98–99
Russell, Sean   95
Ryan, Frank   94
Sarsfield, Patrick   59
Schomberg, Friedrich Herman, duke of   59
Second World War   95, 100
Shannon Airport   95
Shawe-Taylor, John   81
Sheehy, Nicholas   64
Sheridan, Richard Brinsley   62
Silken Thomas, see FitzGerald, Thomas, 10th earl
Simnel, Lambert   32
Simpson, Alan   97
Sinn Fein   82, 85, 88–90, 93, 100–105
Skeffington, William   33, 37
Slane   9
Slaney, River   9
Social Democratic and Labour Party (SDLP)   104
Society of Jesus   37
Somme, battle of   88
South, Sean   97
Spanish Armada   40

Spanish Civil War   94
St Leger, Anthony   37
St Patrick's cathedral, Dublin   23, 32
St Patrick's College, Carlow   66
St Patrick's College, Maynooth   66
St Patrick's Day   82
Statute of Westminster   93
Steeplechase   64
Stephens, James (Fenian)   76
Strafford, earl of, see Wentworth
Strongbow   23
Suir, River   9
Sullivan, T.D.   76
Sunningdale Agreement   105
Surrender and regrant   35, 37
Sussex, earl of   37
Swift, Jonathan   60–64
Tain Bo Cuailgne   12
Talbot, Peter   57
Talbot, Richard, earl/duke of Tyrconnell   57
Tara, Hill of   10, 19
Test Act   57
Thatcher, Margaret   102, 105
Thurles, synod of   75
Thurot, Francois   64
Tievebulliagh   8
Titanic   82
Tithes   64, 72
Tone, Theobald Wolfe   66–68
Treaty (1921)   90, 91
Trim   24, 32
Trinity College, Dublin   41, 54, 60–61, 64
Truce (1921)   90
Tuam   20
Tullaghogue, battle of   37
Uí Néill dynasty   12–13, 19, 31, 37
Ulster Defence Regiment (UDR)   99
Ulster Solemn League and Covenant   83
Ulster Television (UTV)   97
Ulster Unionist Council   82
Ulster Volunteer Force (UVF)   86

Ulster Workers' Council   105
United Irishmen   66, 68
United Nations   95, 97
Ussher, James   54
Veto question   68
Victoria, Queen   74, 81
Vikings   18–19, 26
Vinegar Hill   68
Volunteers (18th century)   66
Walter, Theobald   23, 30
War of Independence   89–90
Warbeck, Perkin   32
Waterford Glass   95
Waterford   19, 27, 31
Wentworth, Thomas, earl of Strafford   44–45
Wesley, John   64
Wexford Opera Festival   96
Wexford   9, 27, 48, 52
Whitaker, T.K.   96
Whitby, synod of   13
Whiteboys   64
Wide Streets Commissioners   64
Wild Geese, the   59
Wilde, Oscar   81
William III, King   57–59, 66
William IV, King   72
William of Windsor   30
Windsor, Treaty of   23, 27
Wolfe, David   37
Wood's halfpence   60
Workers' Union of Ireland   91
World Bank   97
Wyndham, C.S.   81
Yeats, W.B.   81
Yellow Ford, battle of   41
Youghal   31
Young Ireland   72
Young, Arthur   66